The Grandeur Beauty of Idaho

Photography-Poetry

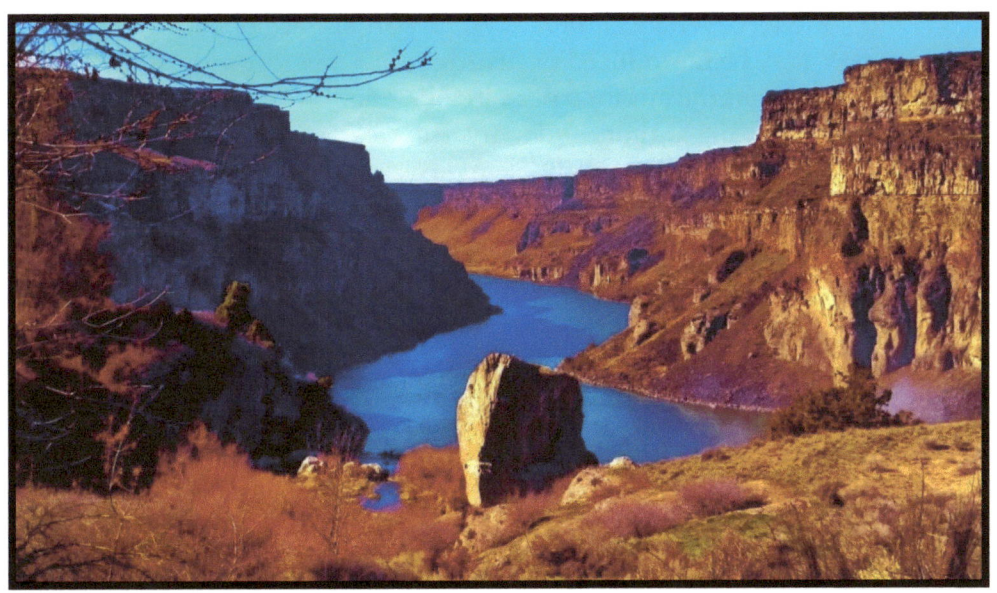

Peggy Leyva Conley

Thank you for reading in the event that you
Appreciate this book, please consider sharing the
Good word(s) by leaving a review, or connect with
the author.

Peggy Leyva-Conley
Photography-Poetry

ISBN: ISBN-13: 978-1542785815
ISBN-10: 1542785812

Dedication

To All those who Love Nature

and

Protecting Wildlife

Table of Contents

About the Author

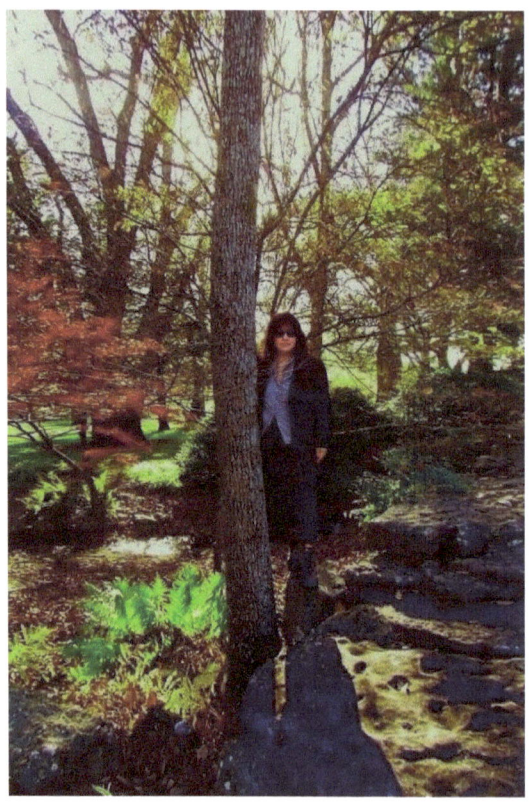

Nature is Universal Freedom in Simplicity

Through Nature is Freedom and Simplicity in life.

Listen to the Birds Chirping in the Forest Trees,

and hear with open ears the Water flowing down the River

as that of a gentle Melody calming the Spirit

of Humankind in the Universe.

Peggy Leyva Conley

The Grandeur Beauty of Idaho is a book based on an outdoor Travel excursion as a Photographer, Journalist and Poet during the Winter Season while briefly residing on the outskirts of the greater Capital City of the Boise, Idaho region.

This is the study of Winterscape Scenes in rural areas consisting of Farmland, Horse Ranches, Lakes, National Forests, Hillsides, and Mountains in open terrain located in various parts of the wilderness. The previous book released titled "Winter Season with Nature" was the first series released.

The Author was born in Hollister, California, San Benito County on the Pacific Central Coastal region that borders Monterey County near San Juan Bautista. She resided on a Ranch and Farm where she studied Nature, and Agriculture while growing up. She also lived in Hendersonville, Tennessee on Old Hickory Lake a Nashville suburb. She currently resides in Rocklin, California, Placer County on the bottom Basin of the Sierras near the Tahoe National Forest and the Capitol City of Sacramento.

The Author is also an International musician. As a Vocalist, she also performs on Piano, Keyboard, Organ, Acoustic Guitar, Flute and Bongos. She has spent many years as a Musician in the Recording Studio working with Sound systems and programs accompanied by Sound Engineers in the Nashville area. In earlier years, she began as a Poet and Writer of Short-Stories, and a creator of Painting and drawings. She became involved in Theater Productions and performed in Plays on stage at Spring Grove North County School, and at the Apostolic Parish in Hollister, California.

She is an accomplished Painter who has shown work Nationally and Internationally and has produced Pottery, and Jewelry designs by hand. She has been published in Newspapers, Periodicals, Hardback and Paperback books for her Genealogical research. She enjoys producing Aromatherapy products, Cooking, History, Archeology and Geology. Including, Plein-Air Painting outdoors, Hiking, Snow Skiing, Tennis, Horse Riding and Traveling over the years. As an Athlete, she has been on Women Tennis, Softball and Basketball teams.

She is a Member of the United Poets Laureate International-United Nations and received a Bronze Metal, and Certificate Awards in 2016. Including, receiving one from World Congress of Poets. She is a Member of the National League American Pen Women-Nashville Branch affiliated with Headquarters in Washington, DC founded in 1897. She has held positions as President and Treasurer. She has received Certificate Awards from Pen Women for performing Public Service and for her Art, Music and Writing works. She is a member of the Order of St. Thomas of Acre in Werribee, Victoria, Australia, UK as a Dame and Banneret.

She has worked as an Associate Editor and Columnist for the Delta Snake Blues Magazine in Northern California in the Music industry. She has interviewed many famous Recording Artist and promoted publicity for them. She has been on MTV with Legendary Bluesman John Lee Hooker, Actor Fabian and Michael Osborne at the Tubes Studio in San Francisco, California.

She has been on numerous Radio Broadcasting Shows for her Music on live Air in the United States. As a Writer, she has been published in "All Star Access Magazine" and "Nashville Jazz Magazine" out of Tennessee.

She received an Art Scholarship from San Benito Artist in Hollister, California. Including, receiving a Bronze Metal Plaque and Certificate Awards from the Santa Cruz Poetry Society held at the San Francisco Marriott International Poetry Convention in Northern California. She has received Certificate and Ribbon Awards for her Artwork, and Ceramics. Her Artwork has sold throughout the United States and is now in private collections.

Over the years, she has worked in the Aerospace and Telecommunications Industry in Silicon Valley, San Jose, California in the High Teach Industry, and in Hollister, California. She has received a CMII-Certification for Configuration Management (Engineering – Manufacturing) environments in the Document Control field from the University of Phoenix, Arizona.

Including, Certificates for Computer Science at Oracle-Sun Microsystems Technical School formerly located in Milpitas, California for Unix-Programming and Solaris-Sun Sparc System. She has completed Computer Aided Drafting (3-D Modules) Geometric Tolerancing and Dimensioning at Evergreen Valley College in San Jose, California. Also at Gavilan College for Micro-Computer Systems, Spanish Language and Piano studies as a student. Other fields of Education include, APICS (Engineering - Manufacturing) studies in Sunnyvale, California and a Certificate from the University of Milwaukee, Wisconsin in the Engineering environment for Document Control Management in the business sector.

Flights Out in Winter

Nashville, Tennessee to St. Paul Minnesota to Boise, Idaho

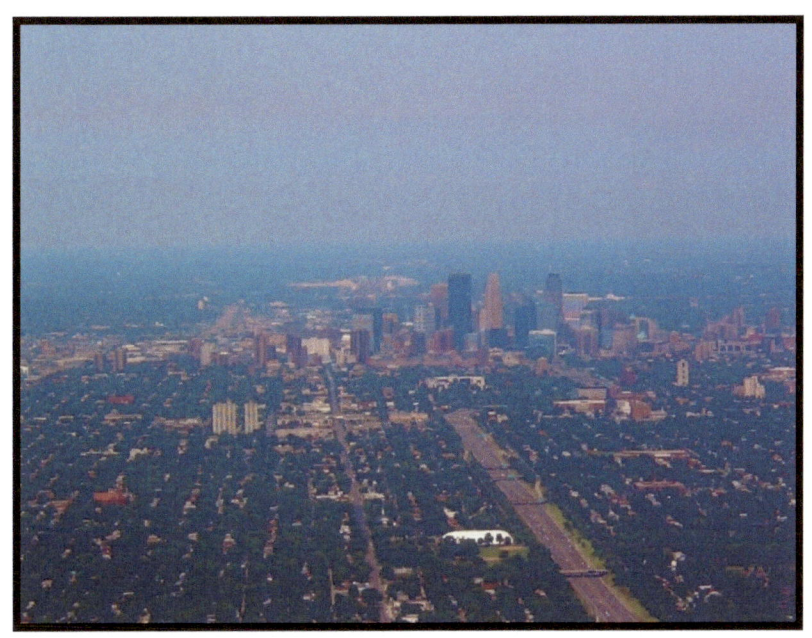

City of Nashville, Tennessee

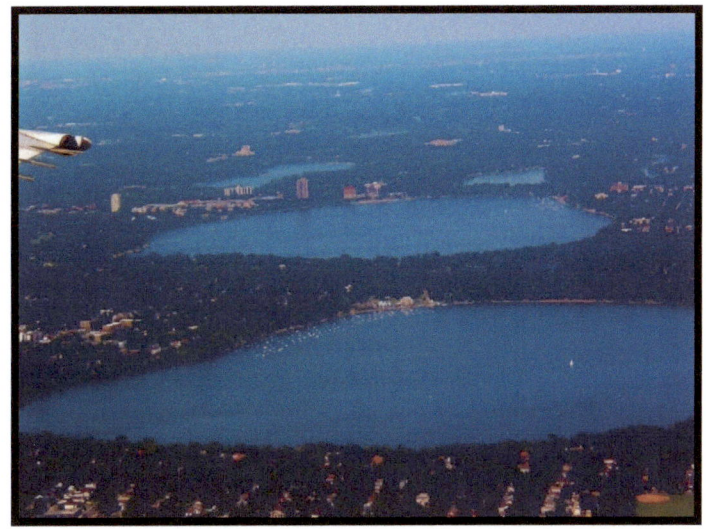

View of Lakes

St. Paul, Minnesota Airport

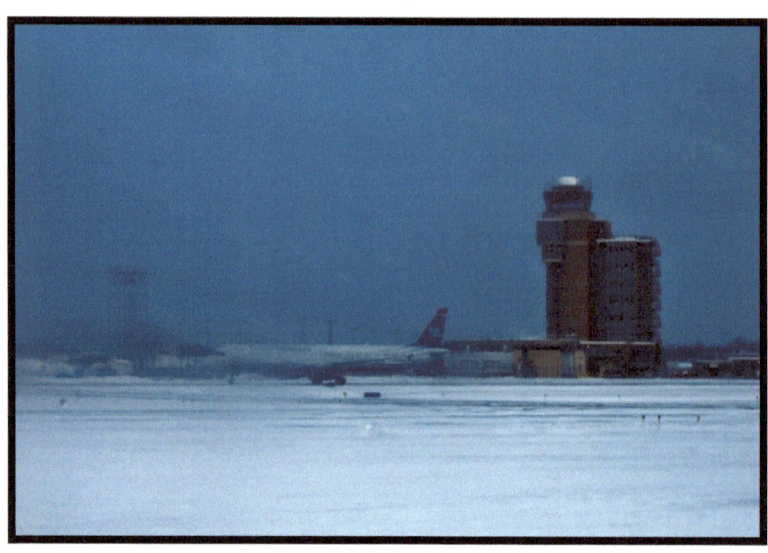

Snow on Runway

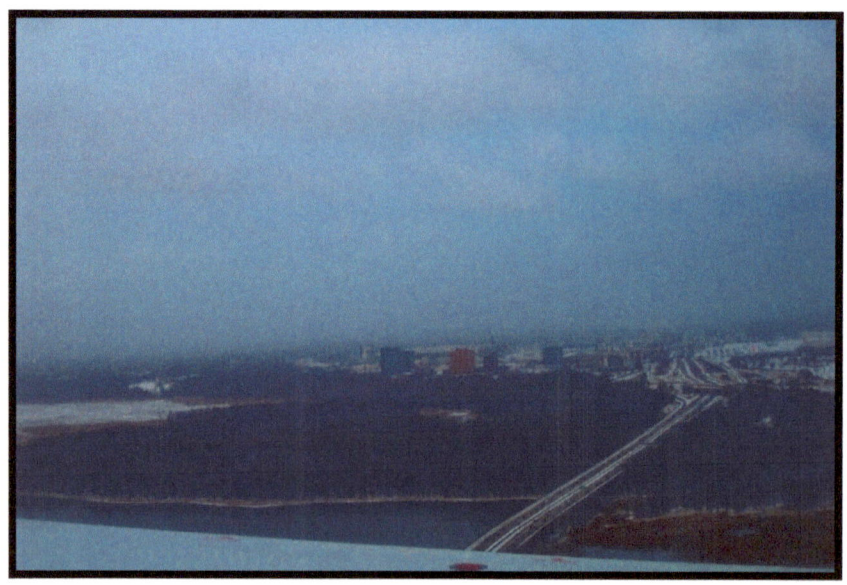

City of St. Paul, Minnesota

Boise, Idaho

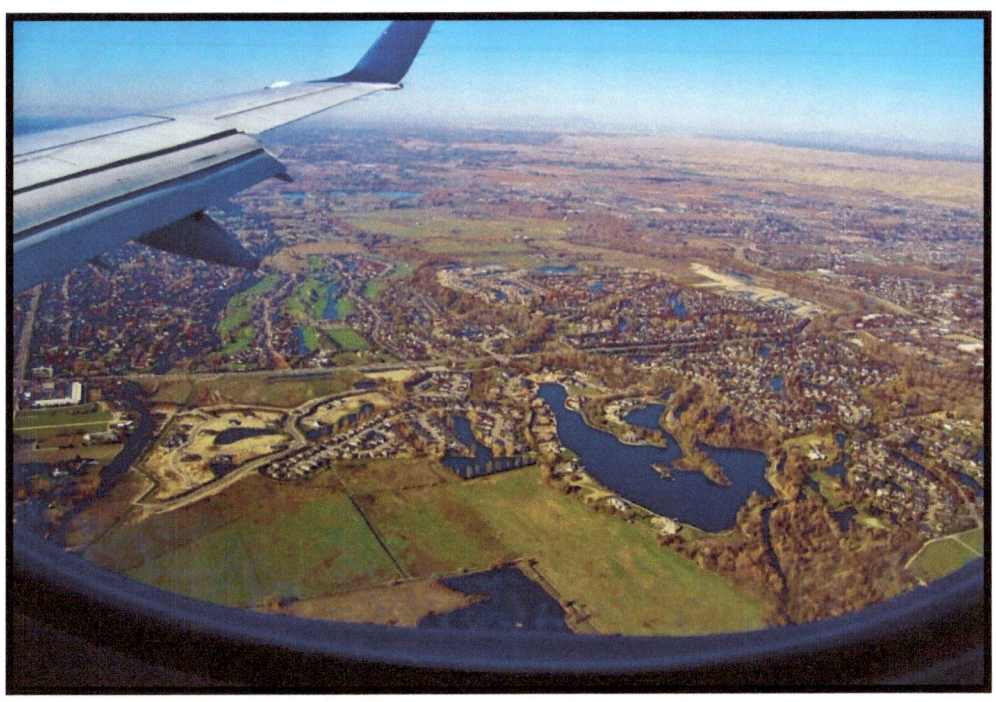

Aerial View – Lakes, Golf Courses and City dwellings

Shoshone Twin Falls, Idaho

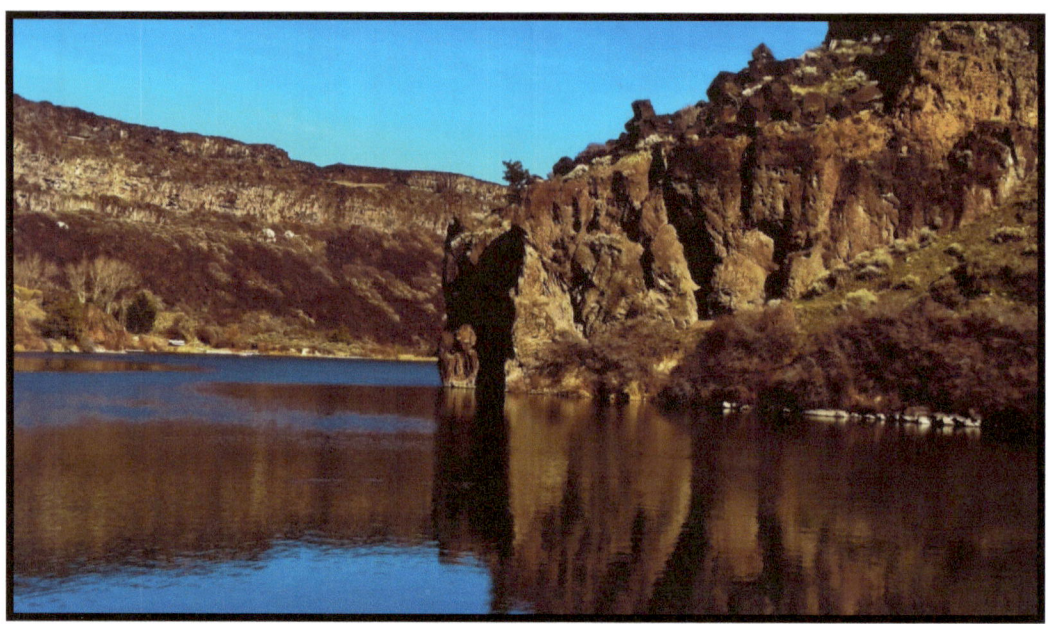

Silky smooth Water

Pointed Rock formations

Curvy body of River flows

Blue Sky

Stillness

Snake River

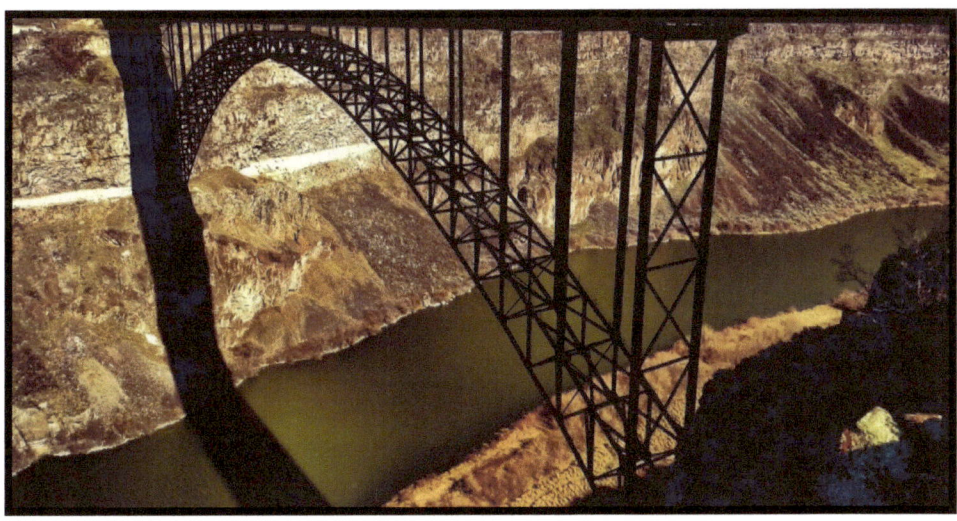

Cast Iron

Strong and sturdy Bridge

Bellowing high above the Sky

Open Air Space

Just below the Rugged Land

Oh' how the Snake River Flows

Channeling for Miles

in its Magical presence

a wonder of surprise most pleasing to the eyes.

Red Barn and Vintage Car

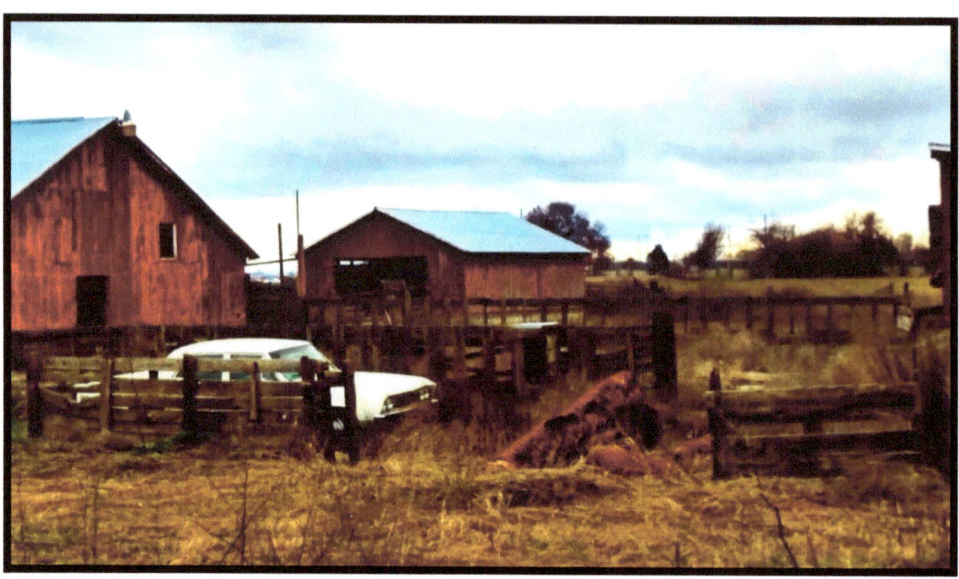

Wooden Fences

White Vintage Car

Early Morning

Chilly Weather

Clouds' in the Sky

Red Rustic Barns in a distance

Roosters Crowing

New Day has begun

Abandoned Barns

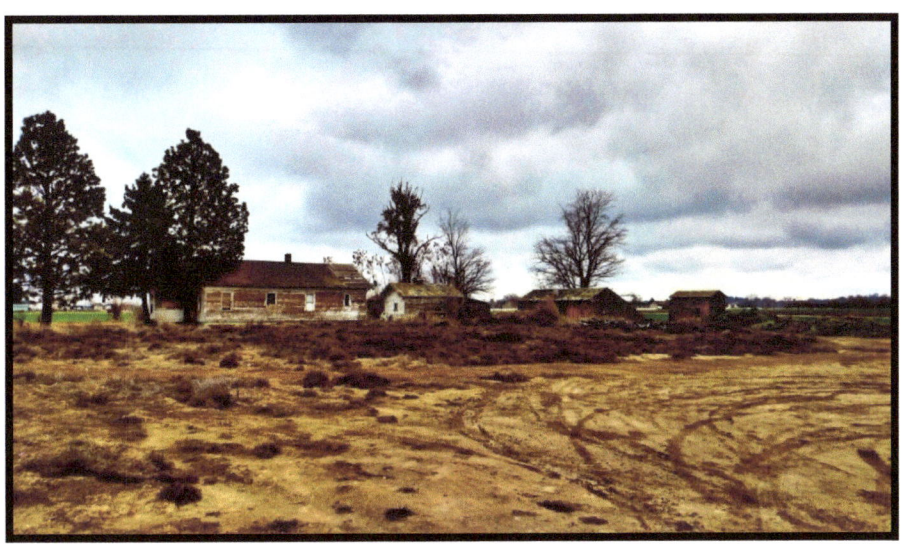

High Clouds

Abandoned Farm

Old Home a place where Farmers once lived

Migrant Field workers

Planting crops on the Land

with Tools in their Hands

trying just to make a decent living

for their Families and Children who once

Laughed, and Played outdoors after school.

As Women stayed indoors to Sew, Cook and clean dirty laundry.

Farm Houses

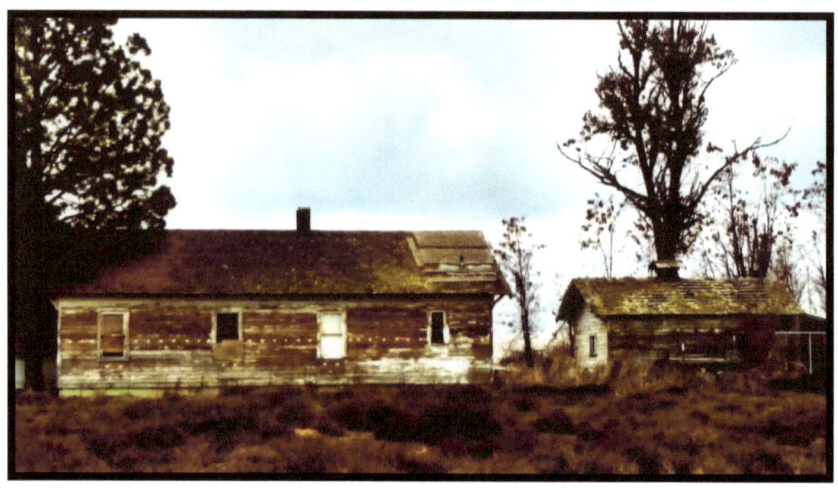

Boarded up Windows

Ghosts of the Past

Leaving impressions on the Walls inside the Old Houses

from another time period long gone.

Dairy Farm

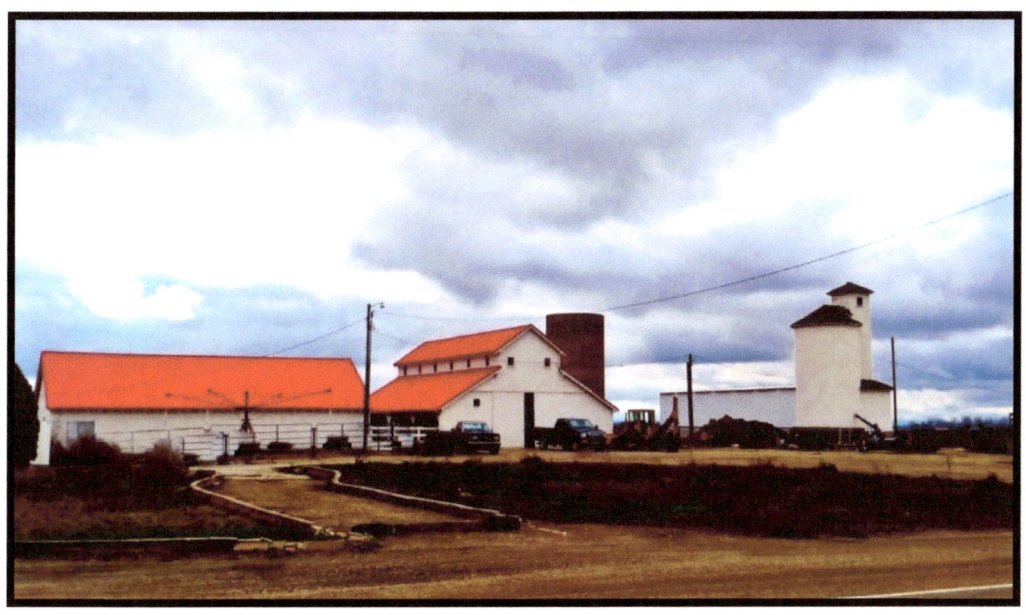

Red Roofs

Country Trucks

Dairy Farm in all its Beauty

Americana way of Life there in Idaho

Long Barn

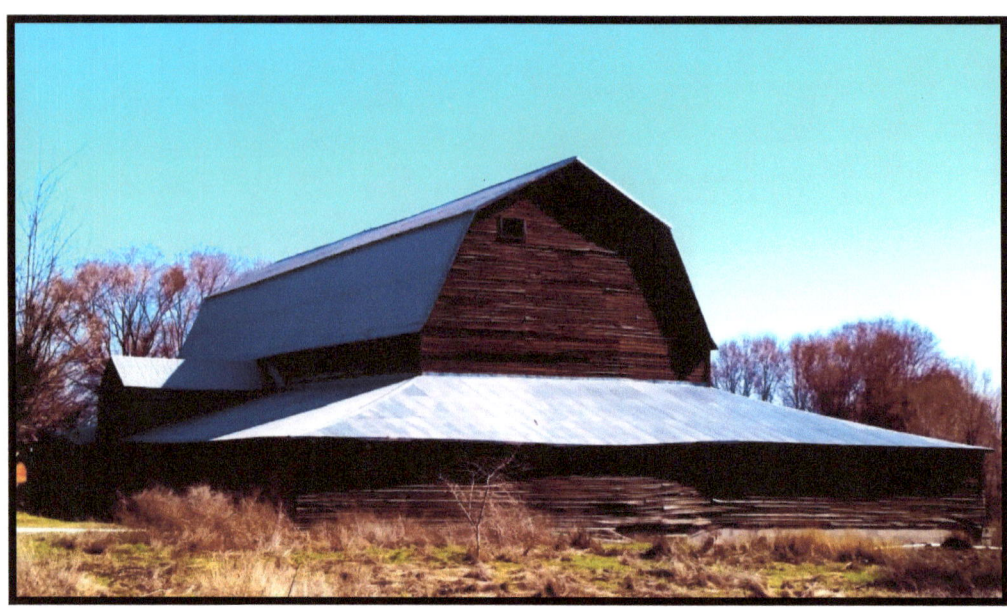

Outskirts of Caldwell

There sits an Old Long Wooden Barn

with surrounding Nature Trees and Tin roofs.

A place the Sun shines so bright

of Memories and past reflections.

As Shadows, fill the Land of familiar Faces

in the Heartland of Mankind's own inventions.

White Barn of Majestic Beauty

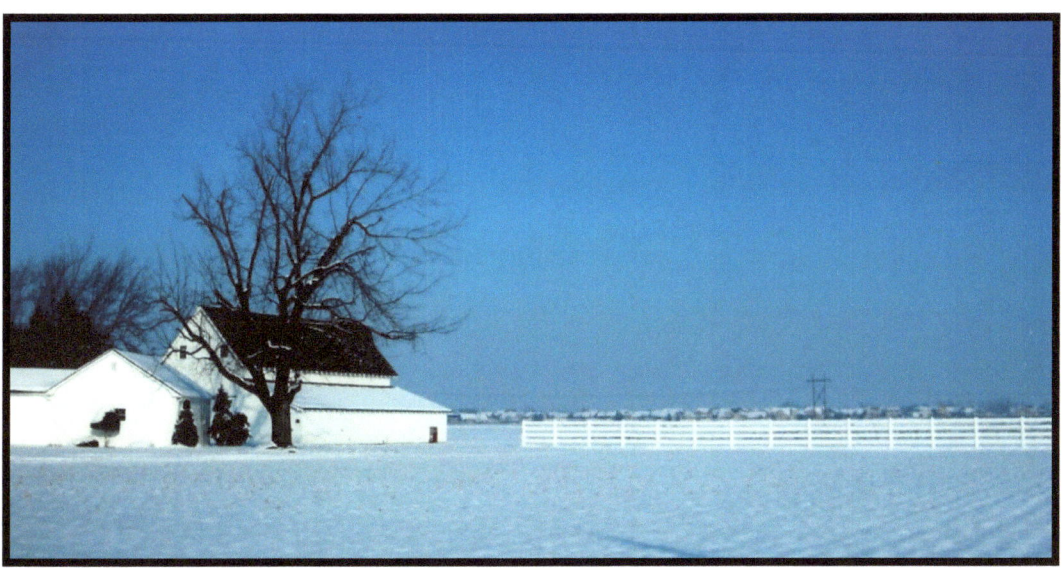

Oak Tree with no Leaves

Outstretched Branches

White Wooden Fence

Frost and Snow on the Rows in the open Fields

Sun out

Blue Sky

Pure Beauty in Winter Season

Winter Trees and Tractors

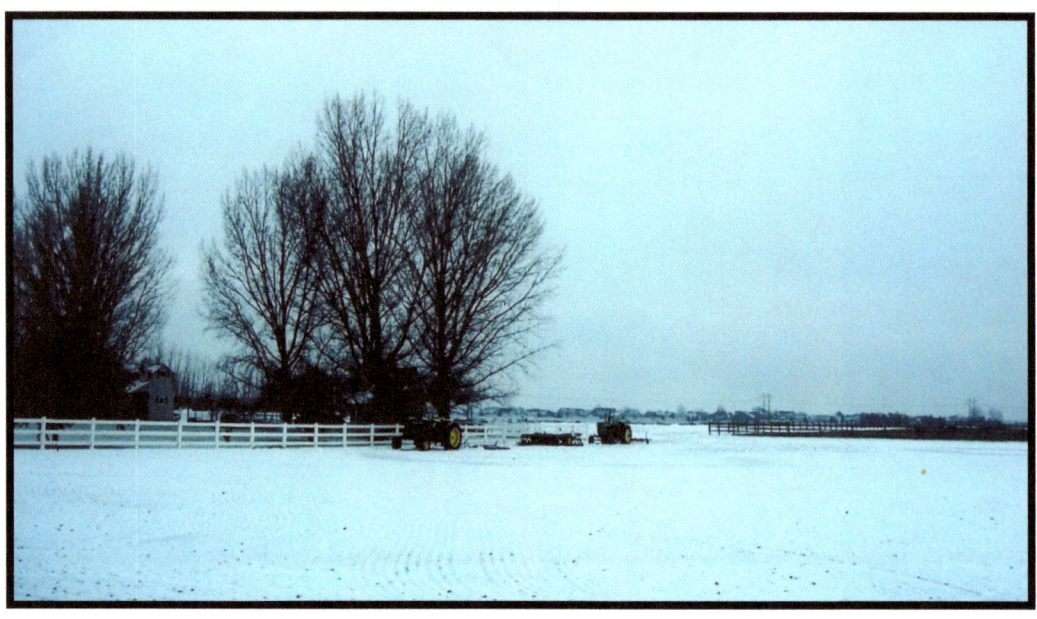

Tractors used for plowing the Fields

Tall Trees surround the place

with Snow on the ground.

Inside is early morning Breakfast where

Coffee is served with Biscuits and Butter spread

with a Knife on Bread along with Boysenberry Jam

one could only imagine.

As all the Farmers sit waiting for the Sun to come out again.

Country Blue House

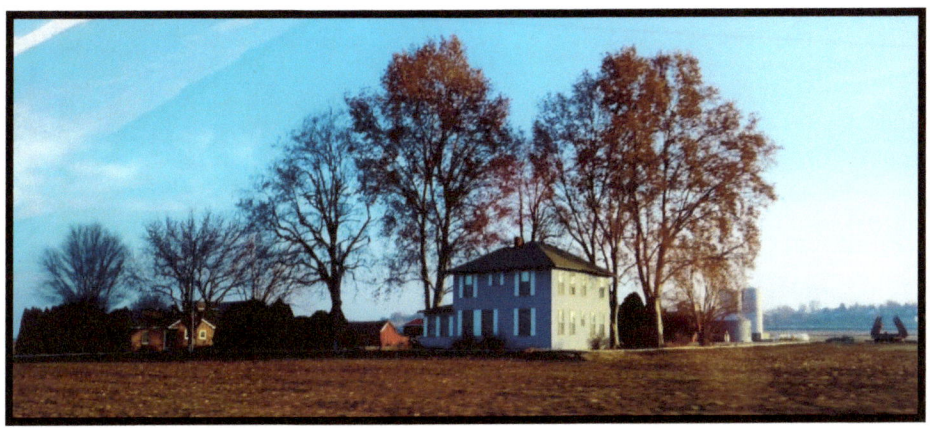

English Cottages adjacent to the Country Manor

Painted in Blue with White Shutters

on a Dairy surrounded by tall Oak Trees and

colored Leaves in Burnt Umber, Orange, and gold.

Blue Sky

Fields with no Row Crop lay Barren in Soil during Winter season.

Blue Sky and Red Barn

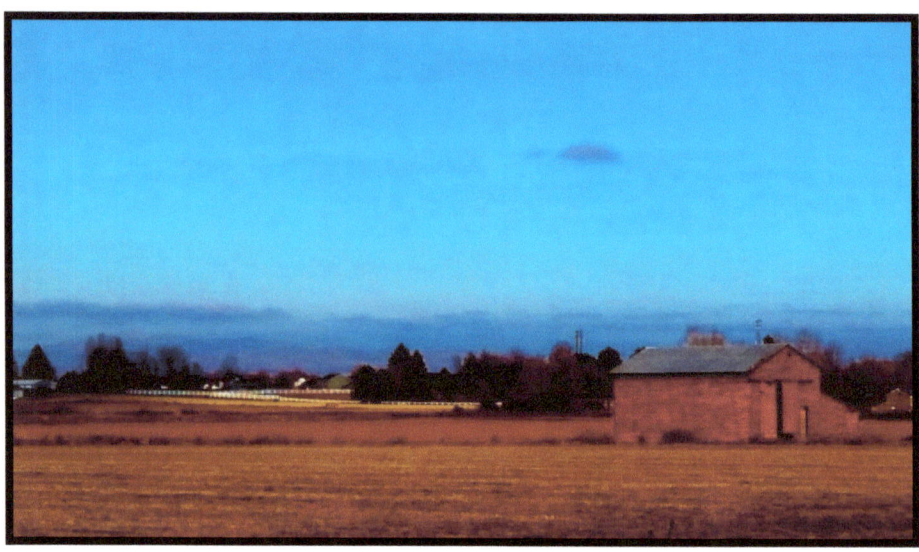

Stillness of Early morning

A Red Barn with a Tin Roof on top can be seen from the main road.

Along the path with Golden Fields and Pastures,

spread throughout the land.

In the distance are Houses and a White, picket fence

left alone in its entire splendor.

Tin Roof and Windowpanes

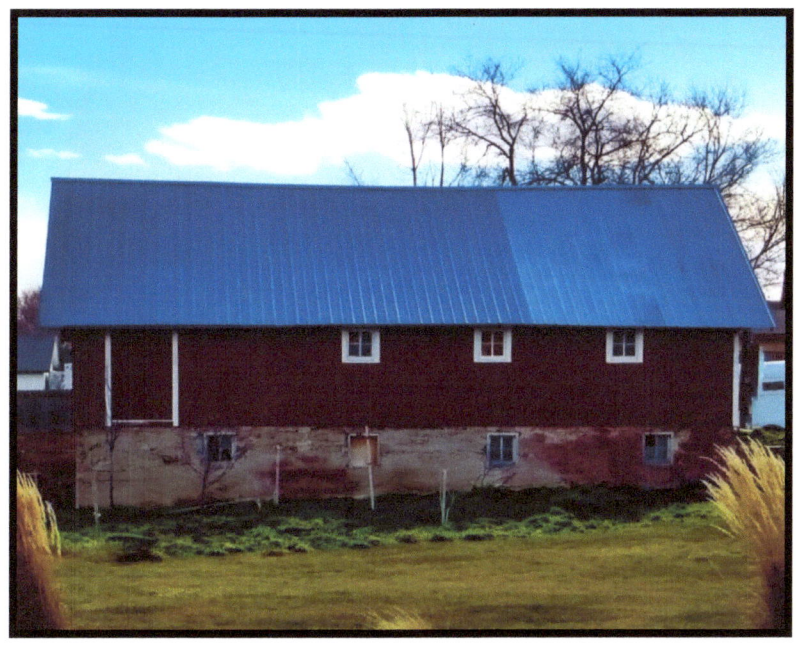

Cellar down below

Stone Walls

Jugs of Apple Cider

Tin Roof

Pioneer Windows of the past

Telephone Poles and Roadway

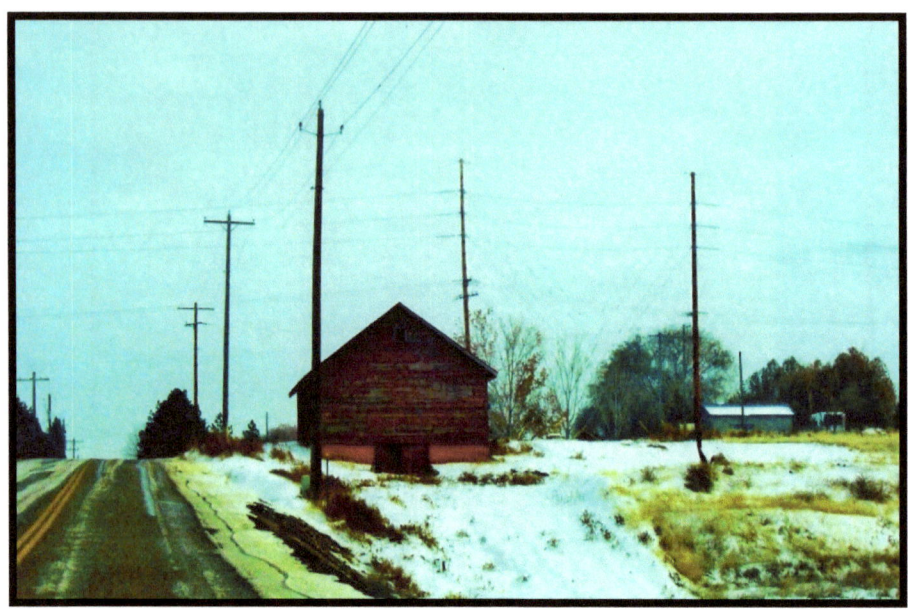

Driving down the Road early morning

as the Winter Chill crept in through one's body

the Land stood in stillness as the

American style Rustic Barn stood in its presence

right off to the side of the road.

It held its own power as part of Americana history

still standing strong.

Adjacent to the further right side was a Hunter Green Barn

holding steady its position with Frost on top of the roof.

The Landscape continued to penetrate ones deep thoughts

of it's rare Beauty to behold forever as a memory.

Shed and Wooden Fences

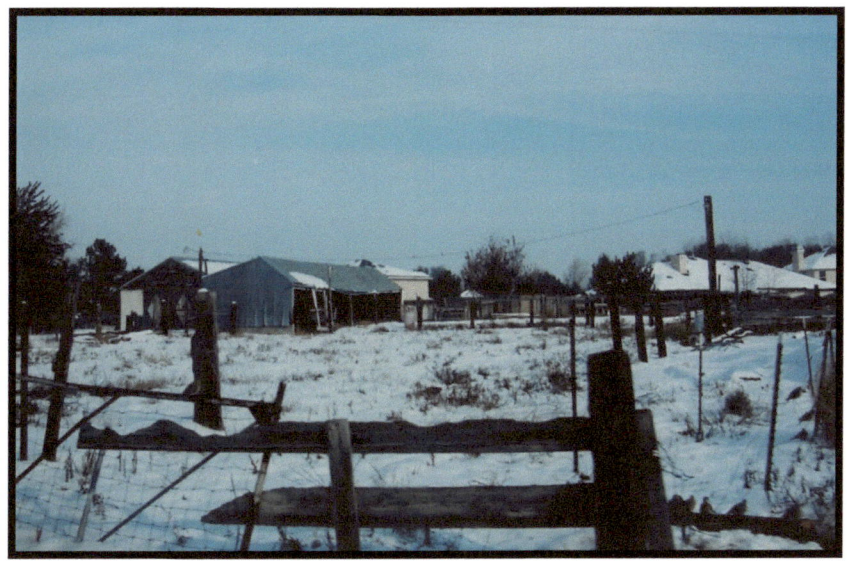

Walking in Hiking Boots through clumps of thickened

Snow covered land as that of Ice-Sheets in the early hours

of the morning one came upon a Farm of some forgotten generations

as if going into the past.

The place contained a presence of those who lived here

from a former Journey in Life as that of a Ghost ridden town of ancient people.

There were no Horses in the Corral or Cattle roaming freely about today.

The Barn from a nearby area seemed empty with the morning brisk air only

calling out to a few, Squirrels' looking for Acorns fallen from the Oak trees.

Corral and Village

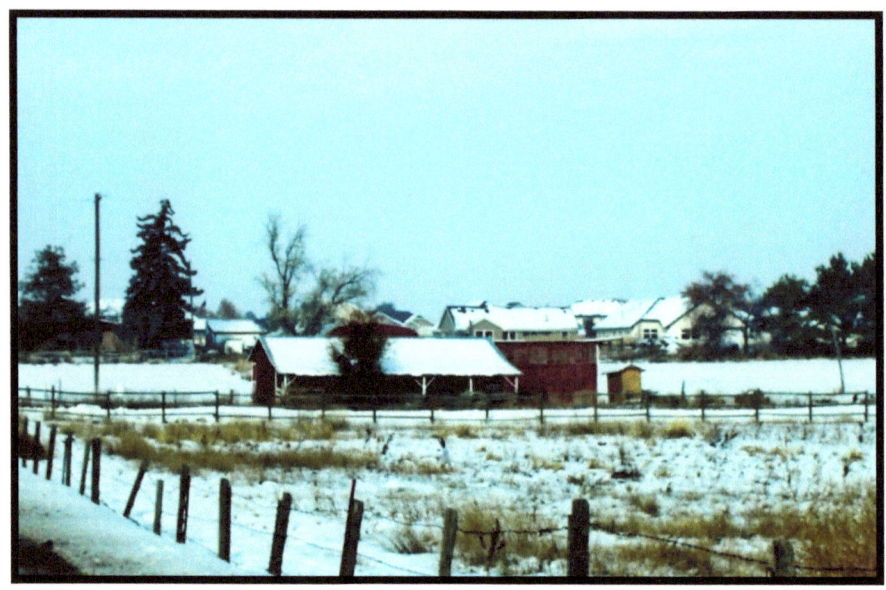

Rural Country

Wooden Barns and Corral

Snow on Rooftops

on Houses in the Village

People Sleeping

Forest Trees

Fences and Country Dogs out a Barking early morning.

Wooden Holy Cross

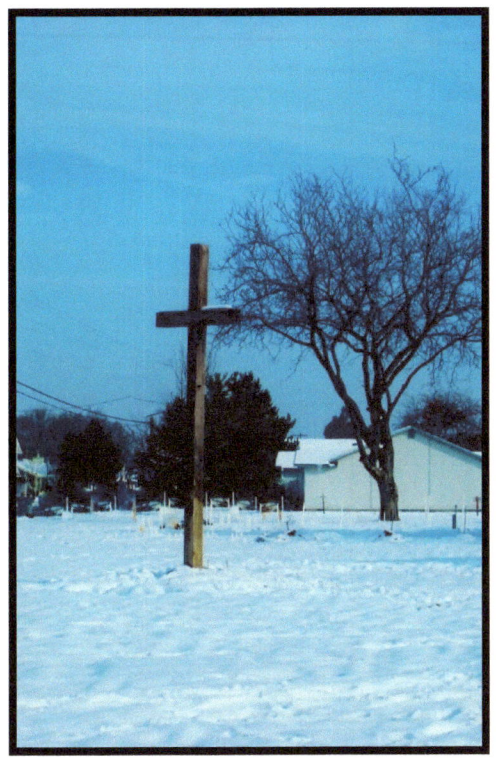

Eternal Love

Devotion

To our Father above

Forever.

Pine Trees and Red Cottage

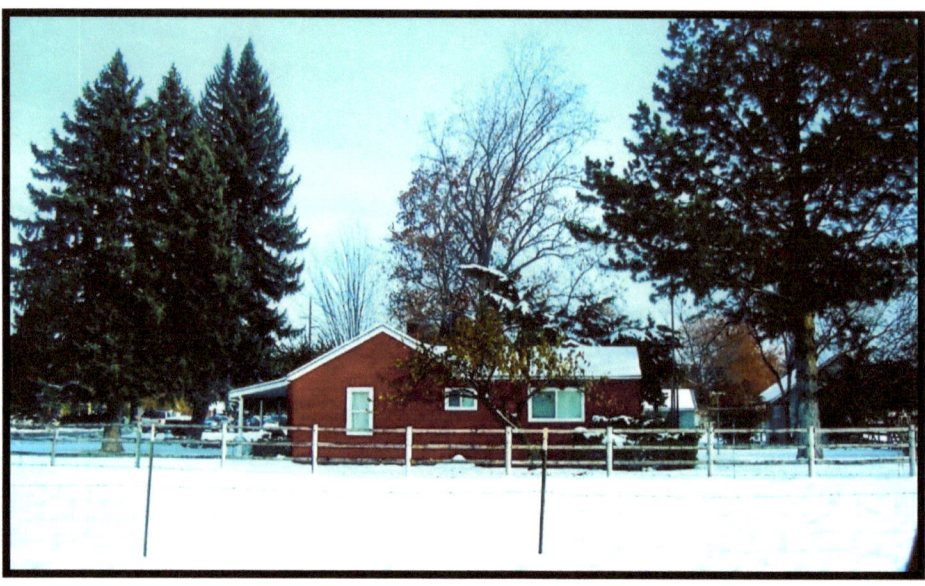

Tall Pine Trees

Snow covered Roof

Wooden Fence

Red Cottage house

Sitting in Stillness

Yellow Country House and Horse

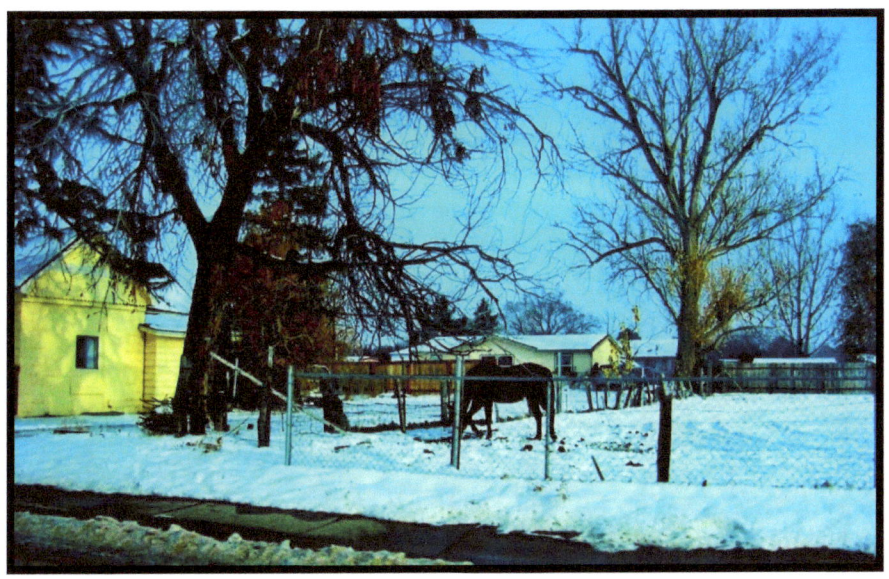

Wooden Farmhouse in Bright and bold color Yellow

American Quarter Horse

grazing for Hay.

Branches Stretched forth on the Trees

as if trying to grab onto Life itself

in the cold bitter morning air.

Winter Christmas Trees in Middleton

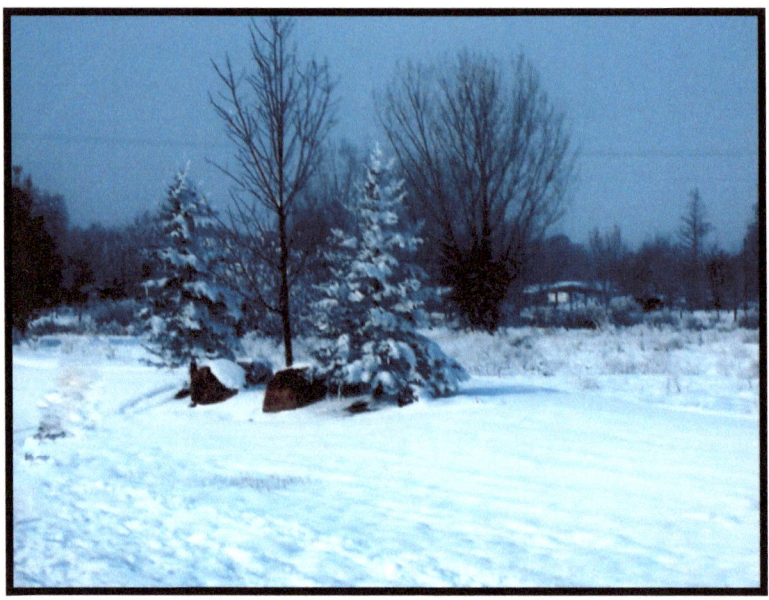

Christmas had come!

One went outside to take a Walk up onto the sidewalks

while Wearing a Red and Black Tartan Wool Scarf,

Black Leather gloves, and a Winter Tweed Jacket

along with Sierra hiking boots to keep warm.

The Natural beauty of Middleton was prosperous

in all that it reflected of such a divine scene to behold

during this special Season and time of year.

Snow on Barns in the Woods

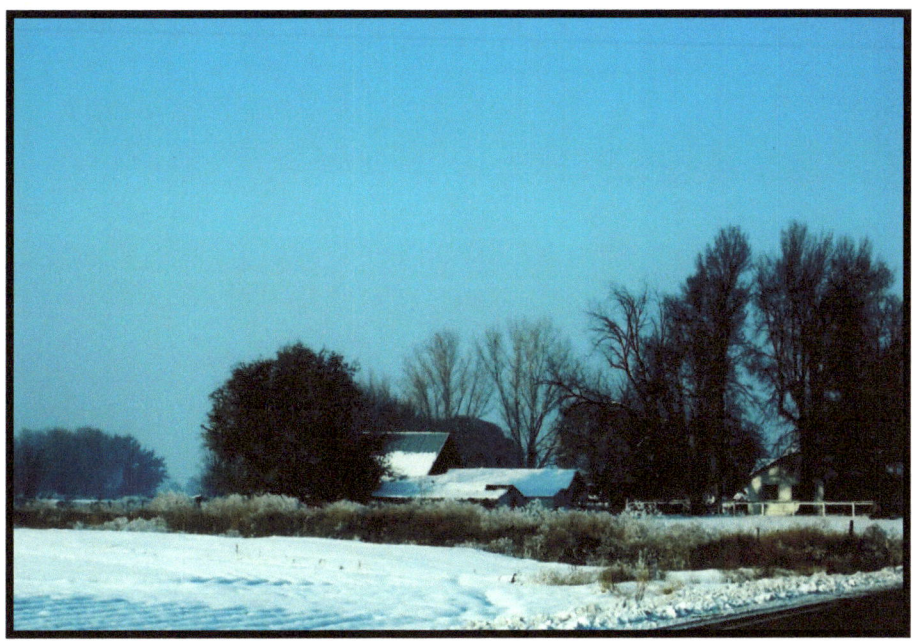

The Barns almost hidden from view

stood near surrounded Trees in the open meadow.

Wild brush with Quail roamed the area freely was within sight.

For miles, one could see the tall Trees and open Fields that

seemed to Stretch out for miles on end.

The Country house has no one around other than they must be

inside keeping warm from the chill.

Shaded Trees

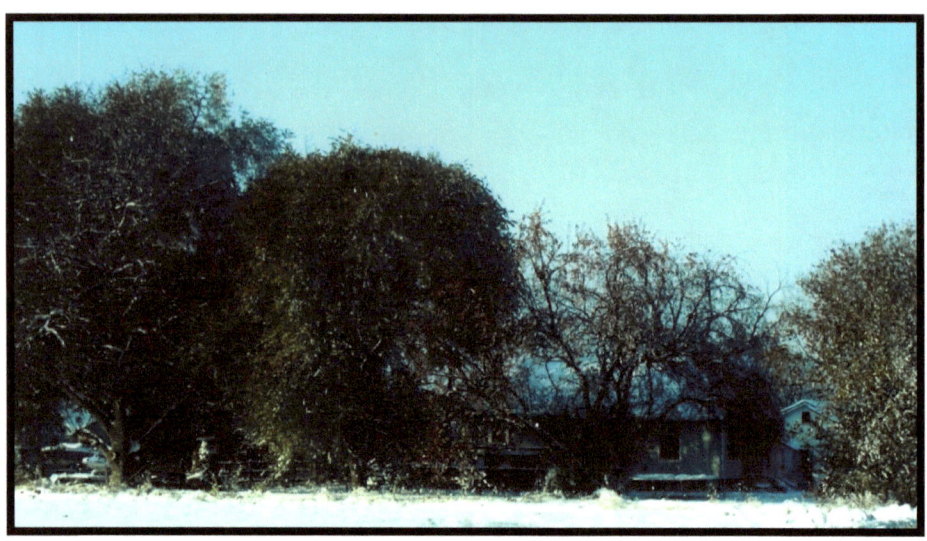

Gray colored Country House with White trim is

Nestled among Orchard Trees

and Fields filled with snow.

There is also a Porch and Wooden fence, which could be seen

within view, and a magnificent clear blue sky today.

Pioneering Farm

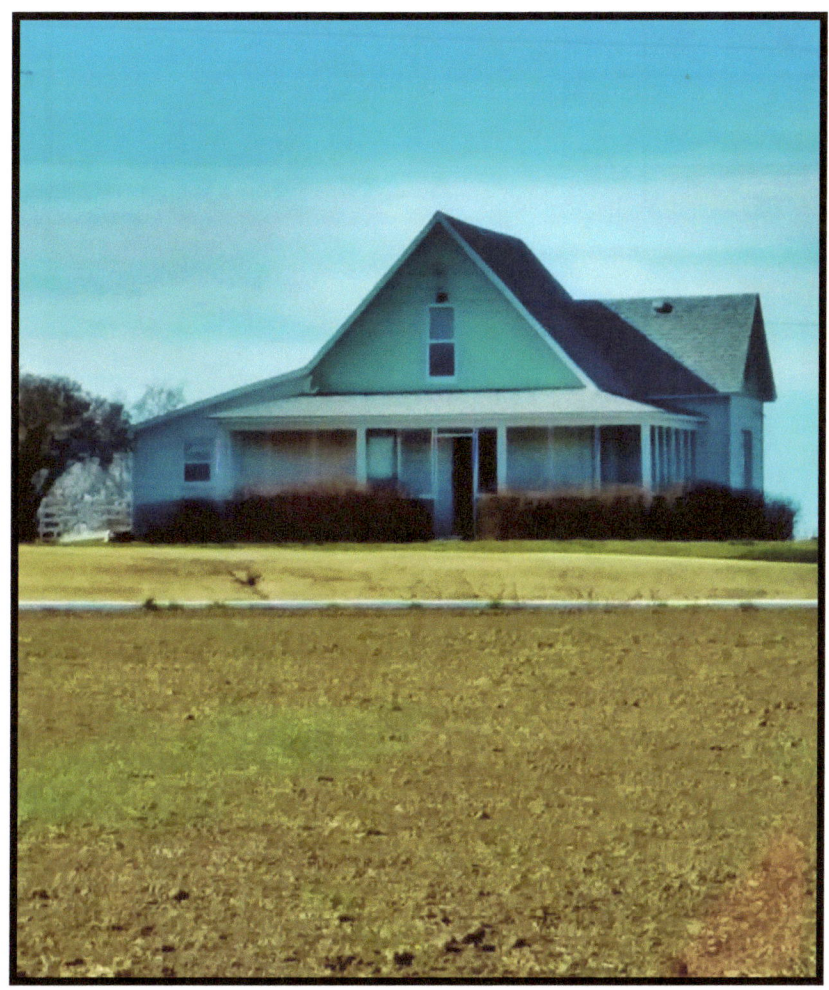

Beauty of a light Green painted Country House

with a Porch containing wire and mesh screens.

The place would make for a wonderful setting for early Morning tea.

The Wooden Structure along with a White Picket fence was a real beauty to see.

Farmhouse in the Country

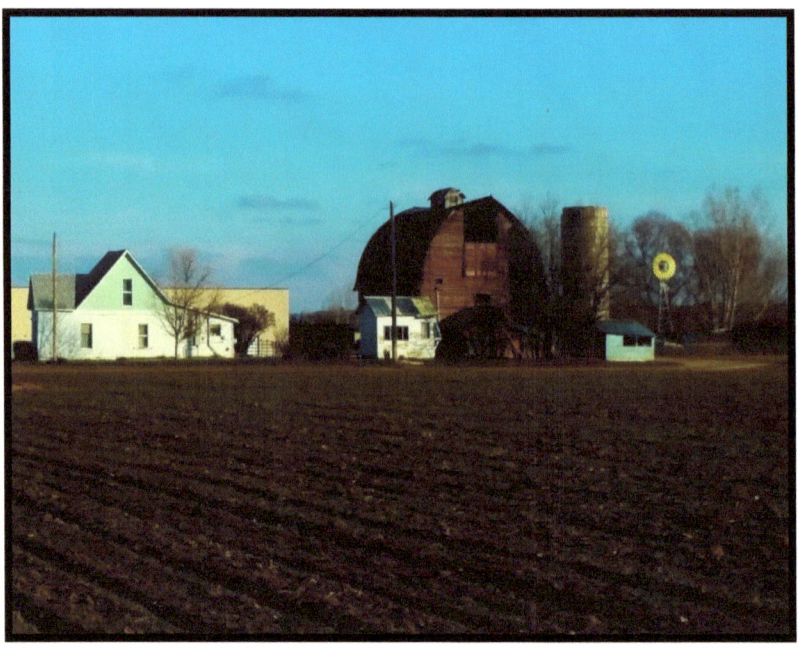

The Old Farm House stood still near the Amish looking barn.

A Windmill could be seen on the land

to the right side in the nearby distance.

There was also a Wooden Shed for Chickens painted in the color of aqua.

The place was an early American style Farm and Homestead

beholding its own natural beauty in this day, and age of by-gone eras.

Tree Branches and Chicken Coop

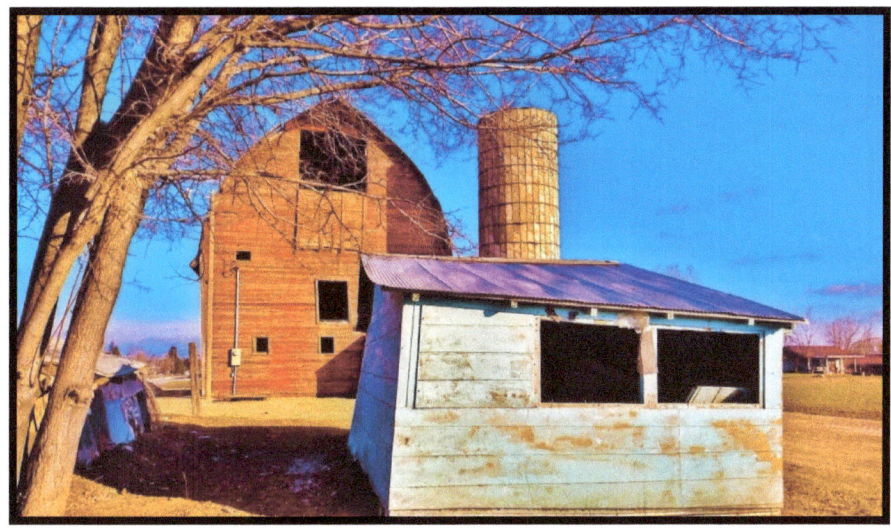

Dramatic Barn

Opening of Window spaces

Rustic Blue

Chicken Coop

Farm and Land of Beauty

Rustic Barn and Blue Sky

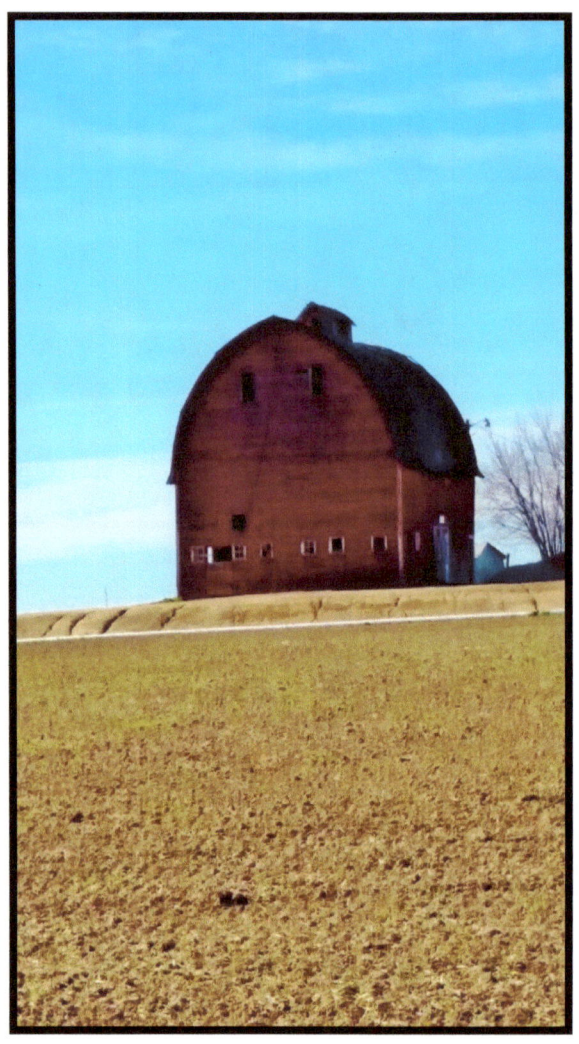

Tall and Strong

Small Windows on the Bottom

of the Rustic Barn

Graceful and yet surreal

Americana Farmstead

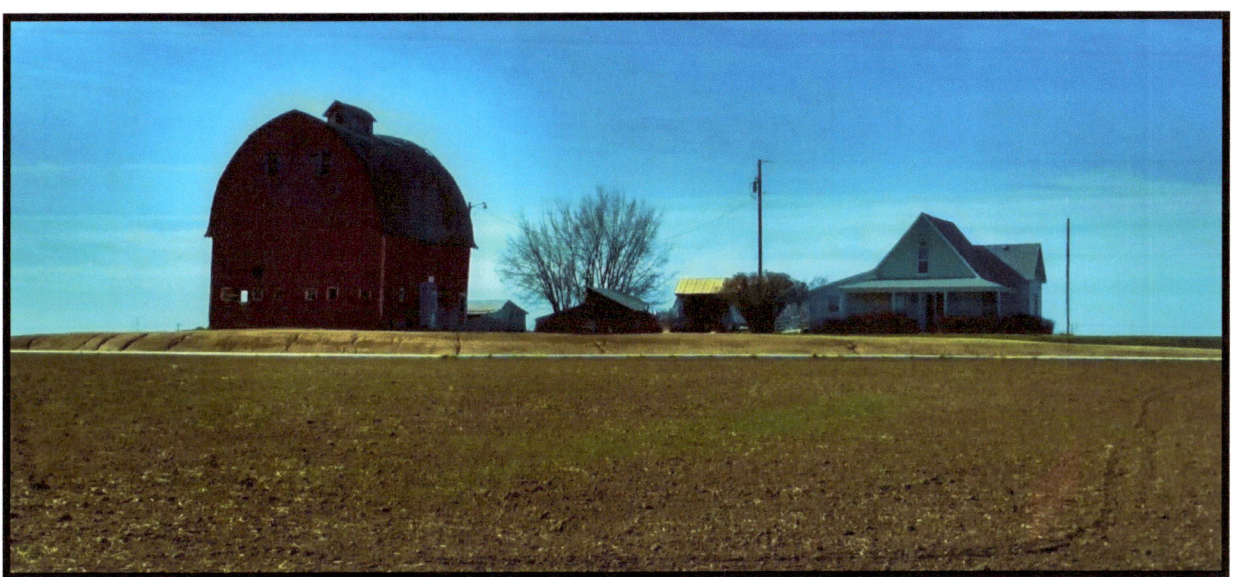

The Barn stood out on its own high merit.

The Country House of Generations who dwelled among

its presence was still holding in pristine beauty to view.

This was a sign that American Farms still exist in Idaho

and are well received by those who care to preserve

Places of historical significance.

Snowfall Early Morning

Red Barn in Winter

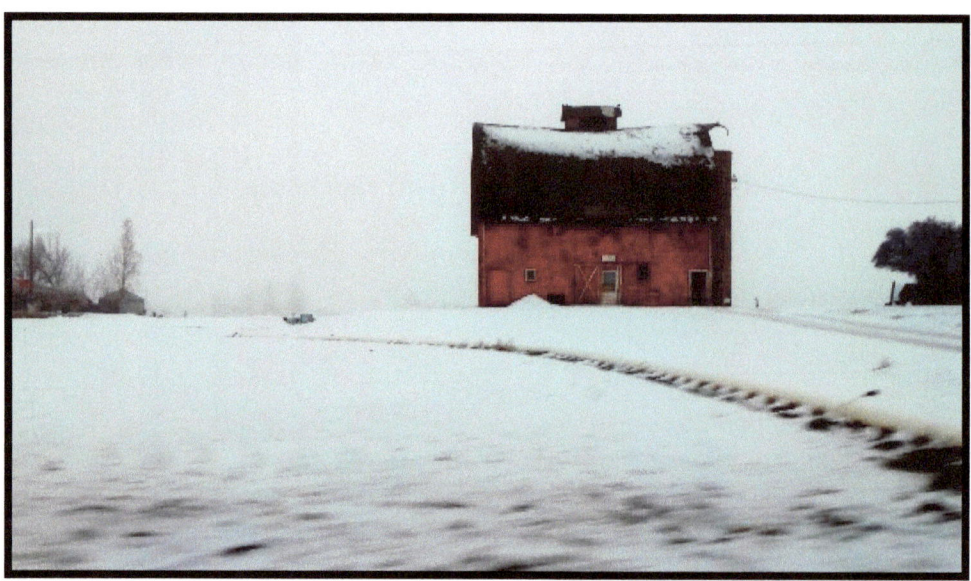

Natural Beauty

Emmitt Mountains

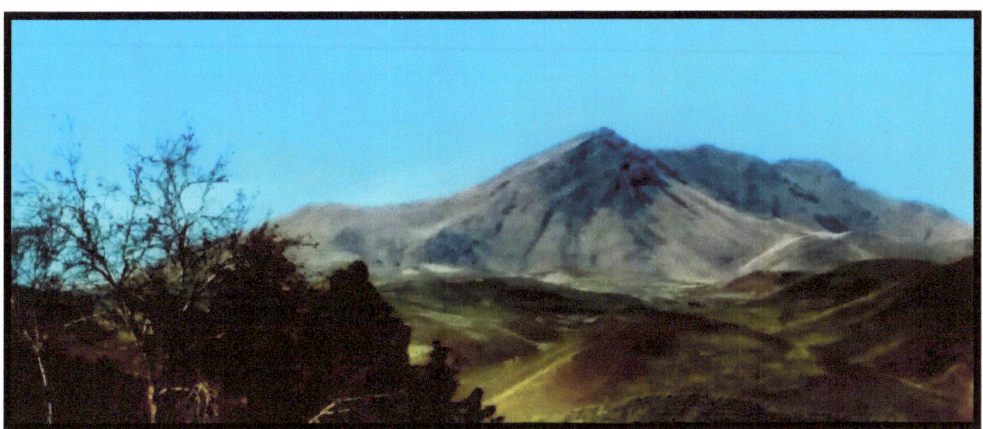

Mountains with Peaks and Black Ash on top like a former Volcano,

and miles of Roads leading up to the hillsides.

Native Indians once roamed these areas long ago.

The area is pure in Beauty to the beholder!

Horses Grazing

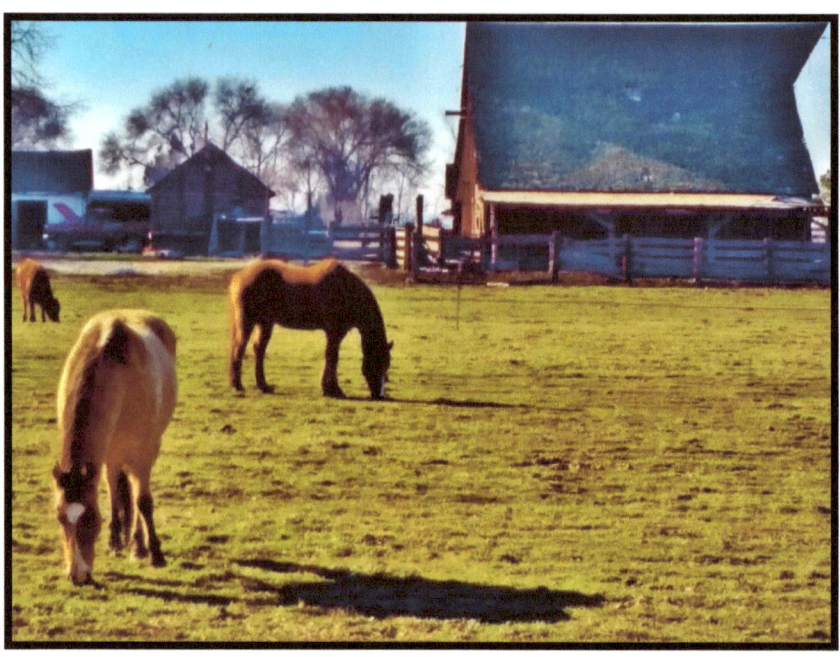

Sunshine

Shadows

Horses grazing on Lawn

Rustic Barn

Country Farm

Colorful Tin Barns

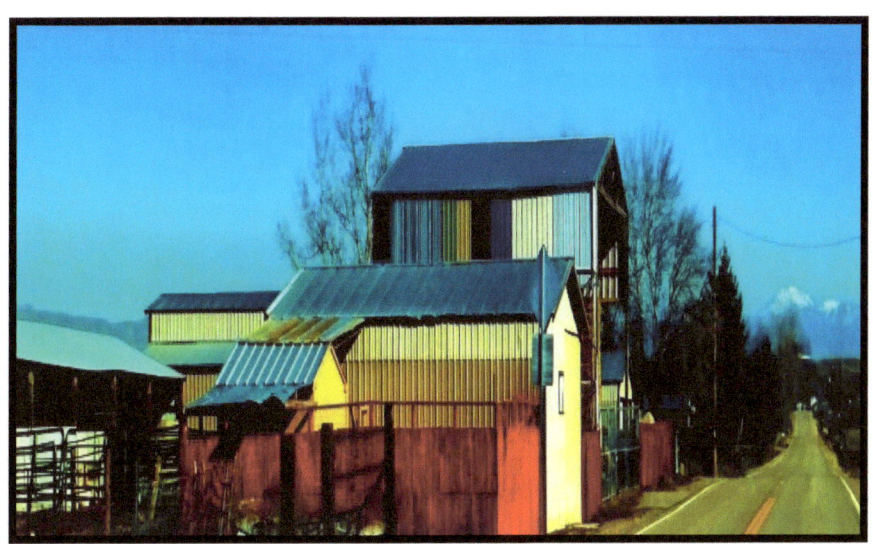

Artistic Barns and Sheds in a wide-variety of Colors

are set along side of the Road

with Snow-Capped Mountains in the

distance, and Farms are seen within view.

Cattle Grazing on Hillside

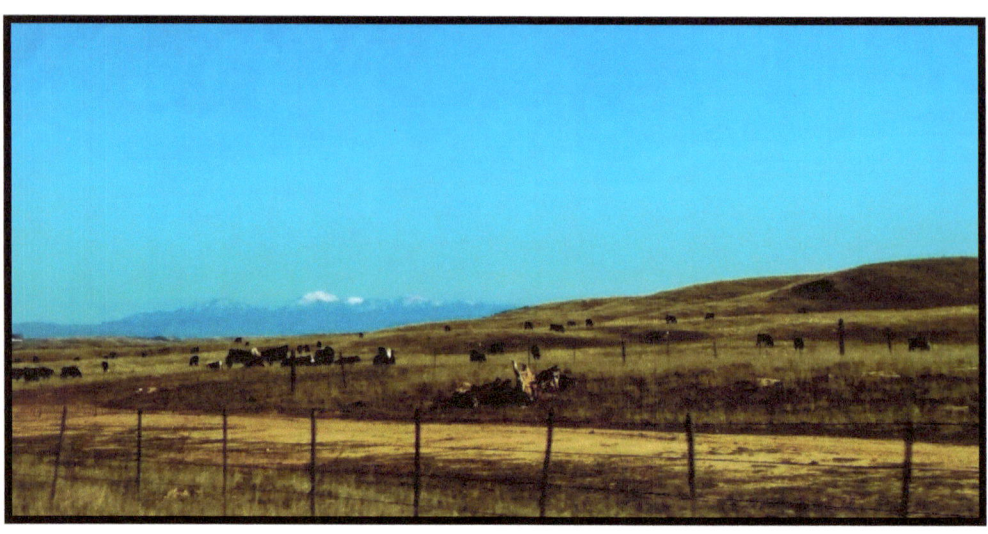

In the Distance are Snow-Capped Mountains and Peaks

that could be seen from the road.

Wooden Fences and Cattle Grazing

stood within view.

Blue Sky

Hillsides

are Peaceful in the Valley

Agriculture Fields in Nampa

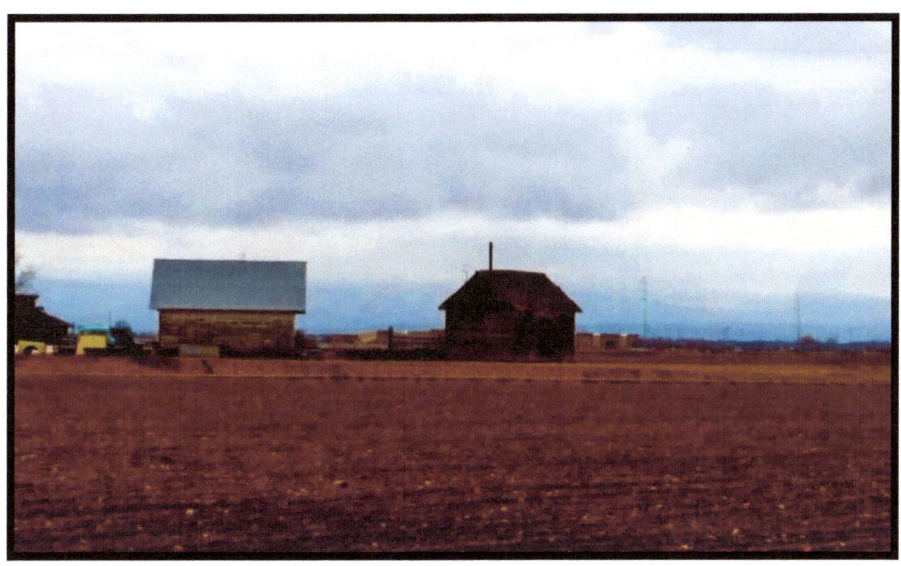

Blue Sky

Clouds

Farming Equipment

Wooden Barns

Rich Soil

Land of immense beauty.

Farming Hay Truck

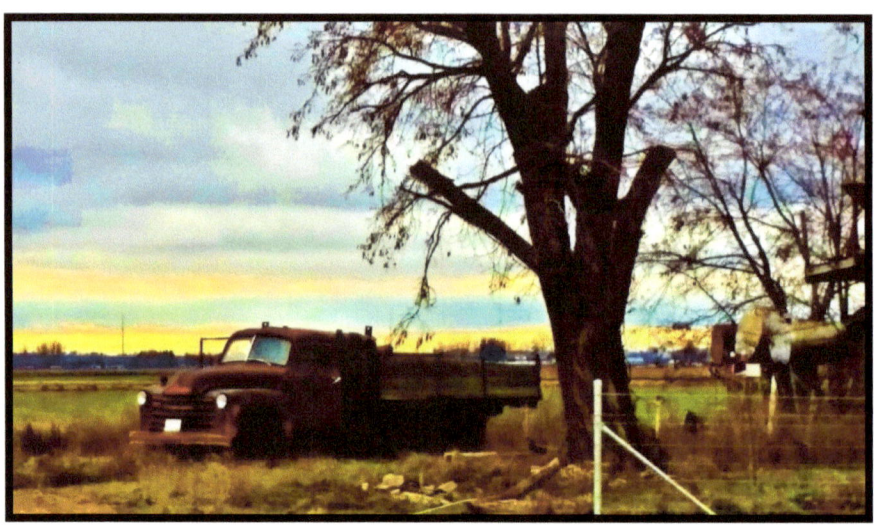

Rustic Truck

Pine Tree

Old Barns

Evening coming

Sky and Clouds

Stillness

Green Doors and Windows

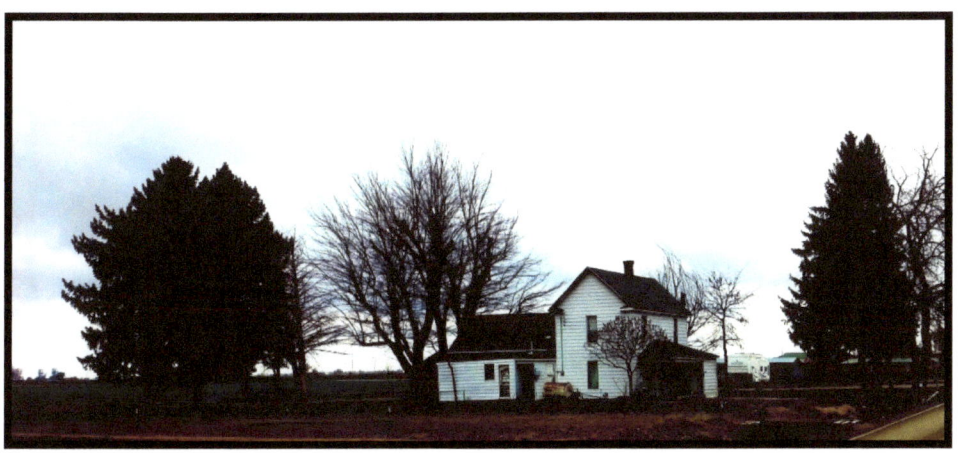

Two-Story White Country House

Green Trim on Windows and Doors

Pine Trees

Crops in the Field

Rich Soil

Barns and Sheds

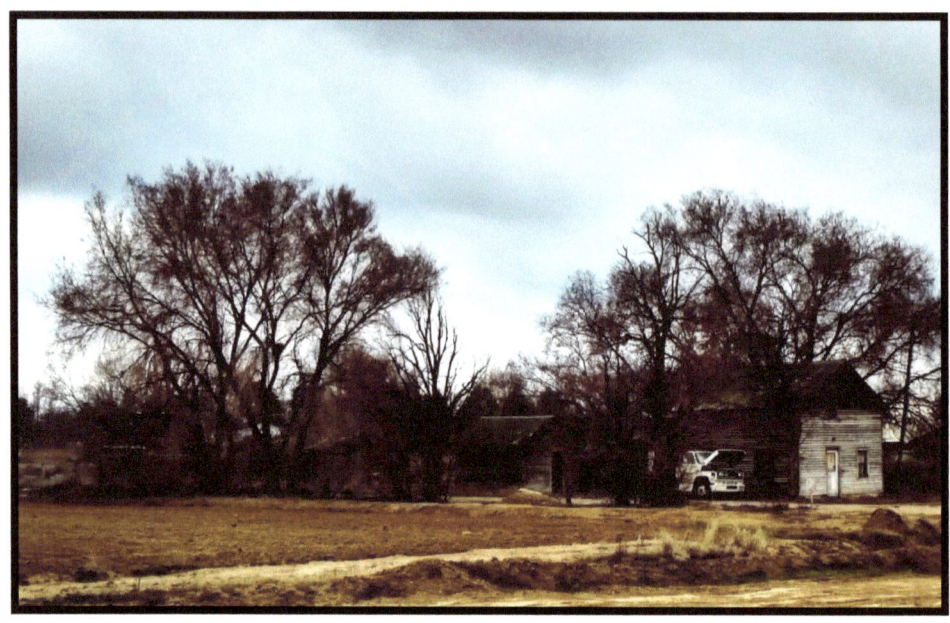

From the Road not far from Middleton

is an amazing view of a Rustic Barn

and Tool shed surrounded by many trees.

It holds its natural beauty just as it is untouched in simplicity.

Wild Bird in Caldwell

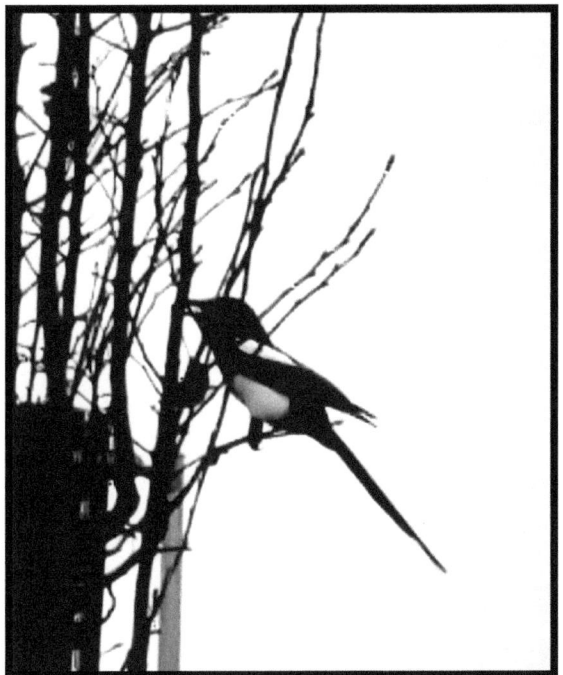

The State of Idaho is known for having many Bird species.

This includes Cattle and Horse Ranches.

This Bird was up early eating in the Caldwell area.

Prosperous Soil

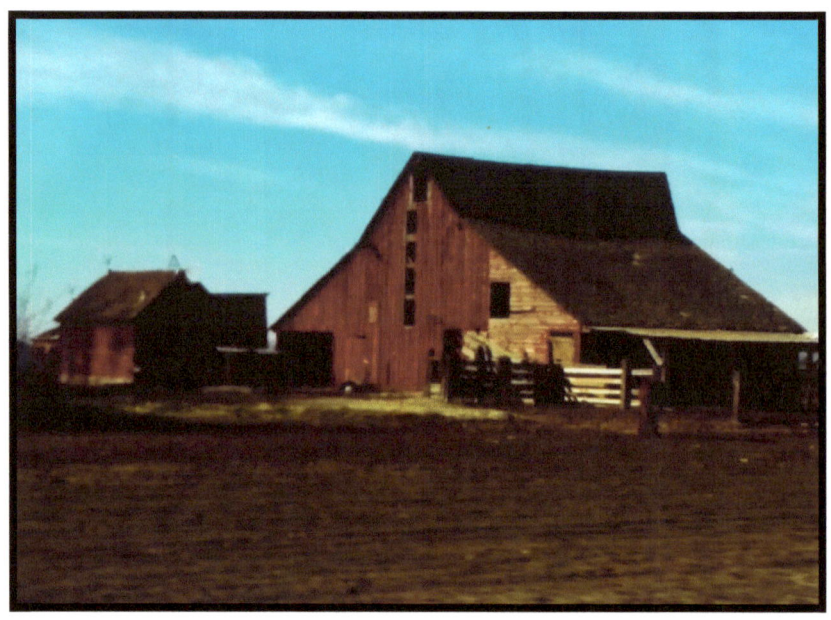

Rustic Wooden Barn

Dirt and Soil

Fields

Empty

Blue Sky

Early Afternoon

Row Crops and Farm in Emmit

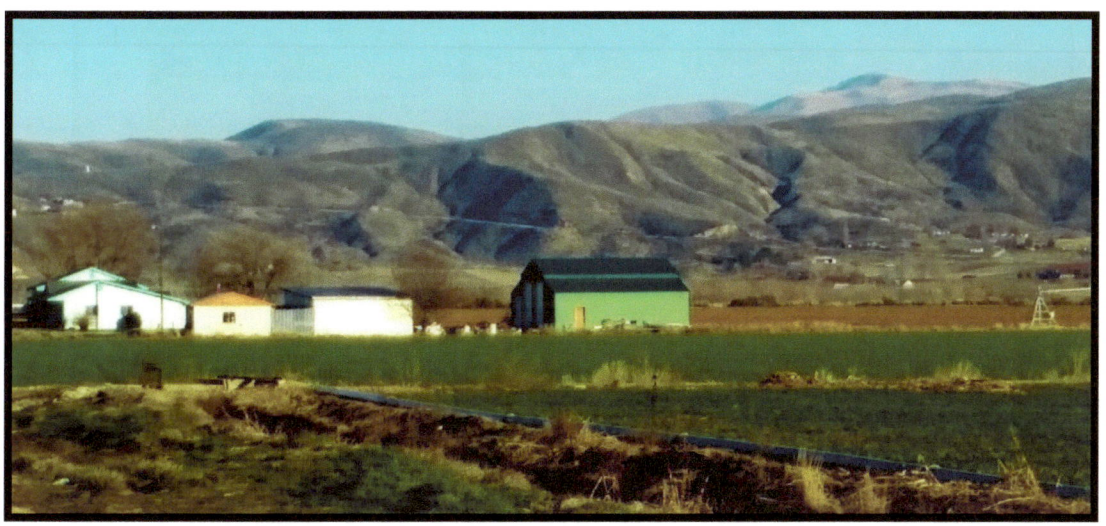

The area of Emmitt is beautiful.

On the roads leading in are outstanding Farms and Agriculture to view.

Included, in the area are Mountains and hillsides.

Row Crops and Irrigation Pipes could be seen,

and White Country Houses with Green trim.

Hillsides and Fields

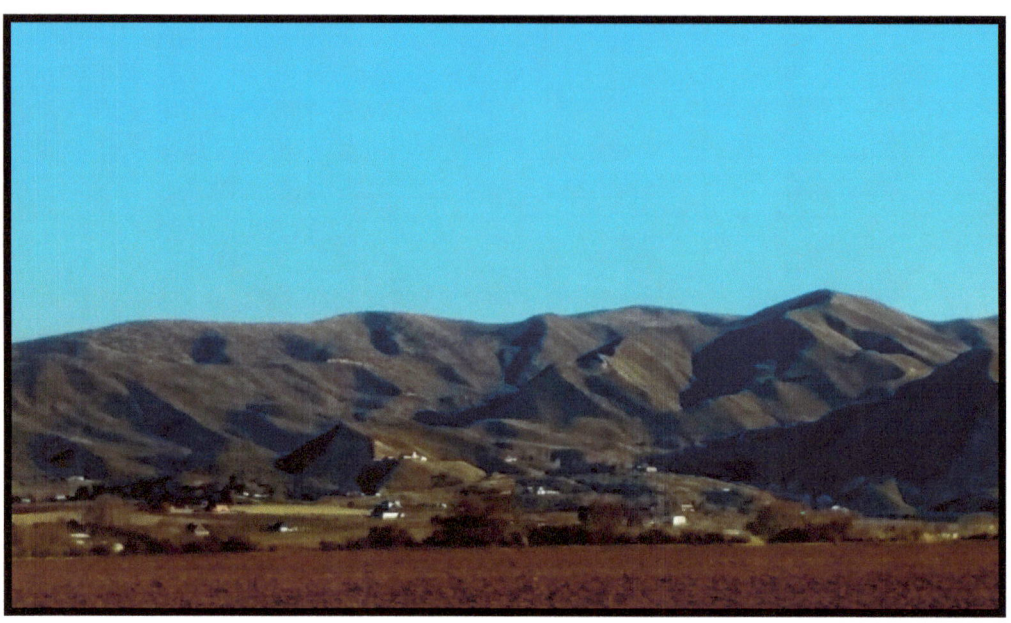

Soiled Land

Open Fields

Country Houses scattered among beauty

Strong

Depth

of the Hillsides penetrates all who sees its beauty.

Hydroelectric Plant

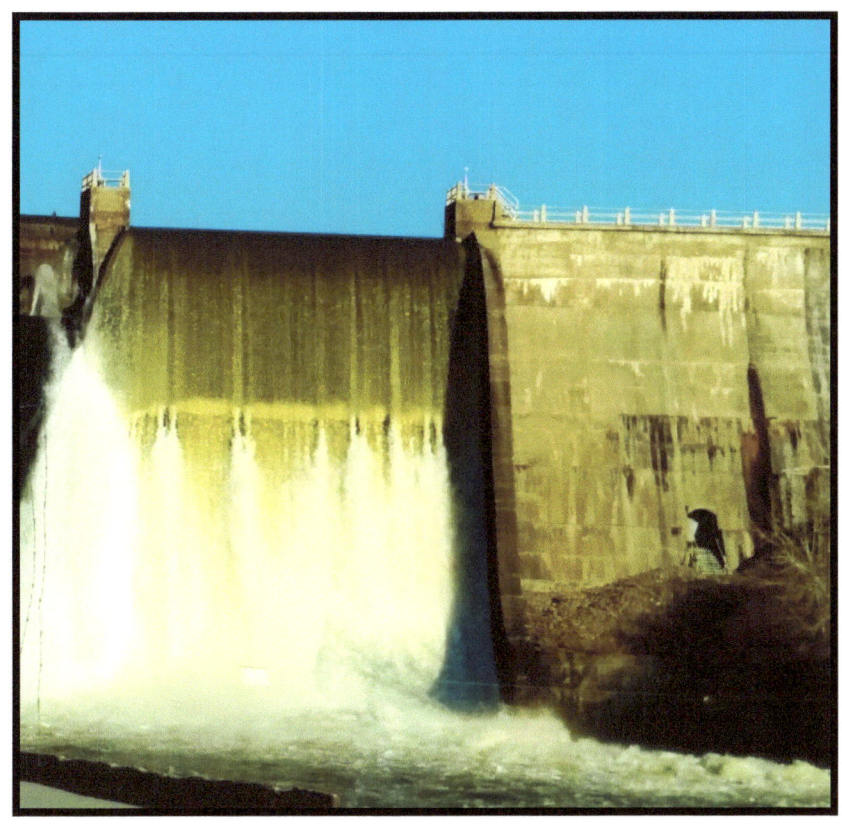

Mighty rushing Water

Flowing down the Channel

on a Cool Winters day.

Long Barn and Cattle

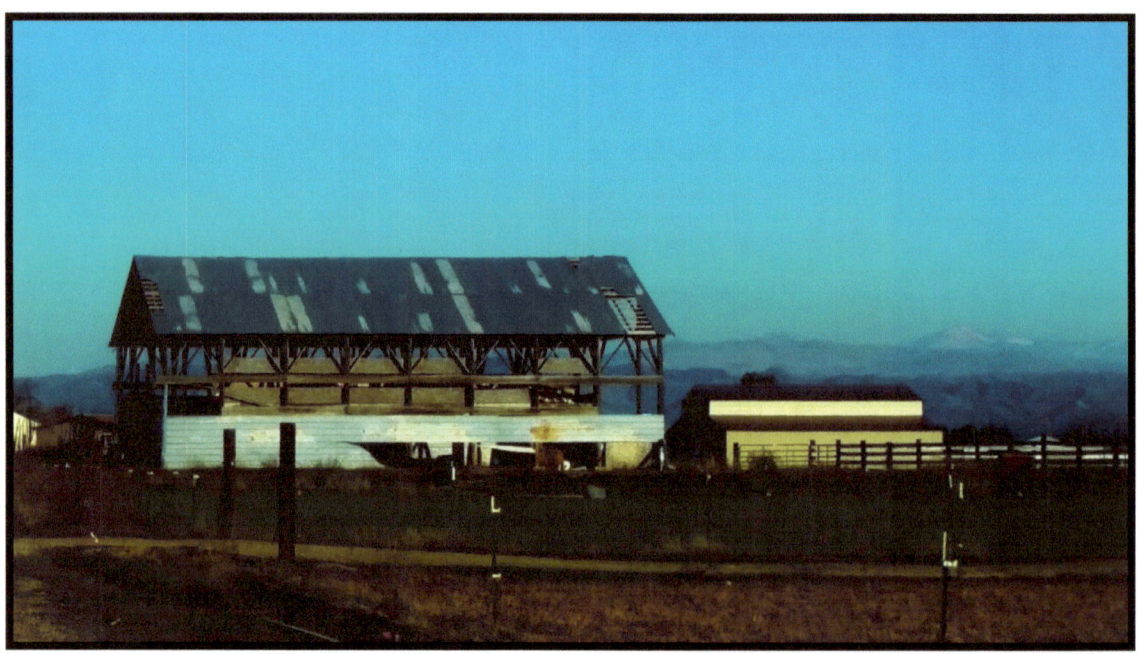

Aluminum Rooftop on a Barn

with Blue, painted Wooden panels can be seen.

There is Horses Grazing on the other side

of the Barns with Cattle nearby on the hillsides.

Wild Brush and Red Barn

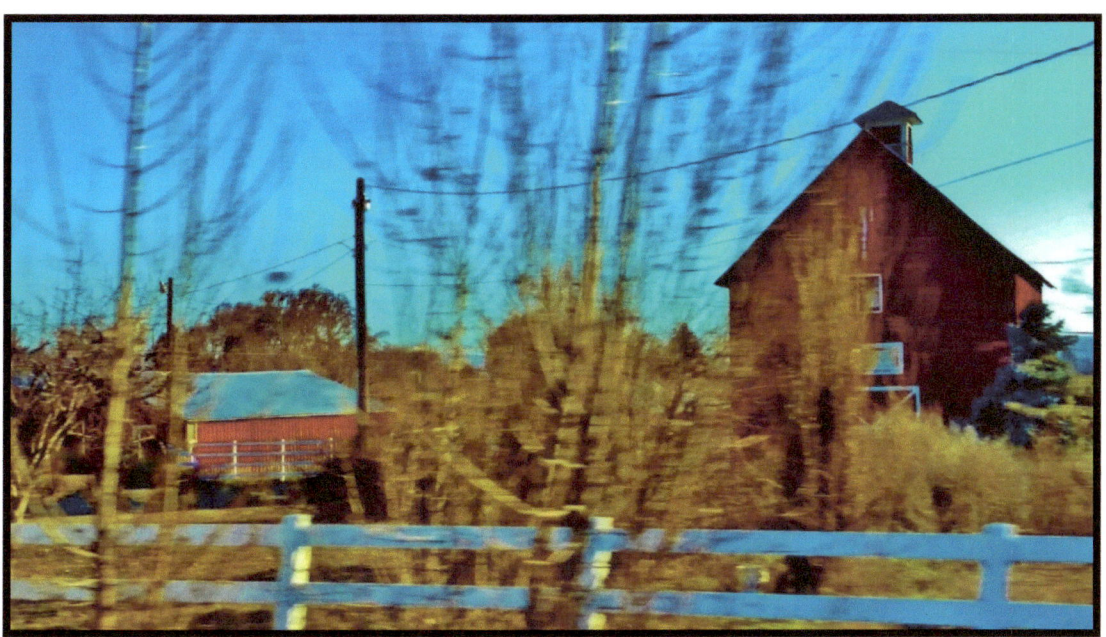

Country Farm House with a Bell Tower on top

White Picket Fence

Red Barn for Horses and Cattle

Telephone Poles

Tree Branches

Wind

Stirring up a new day

Sun Rays upon the Land in Boise

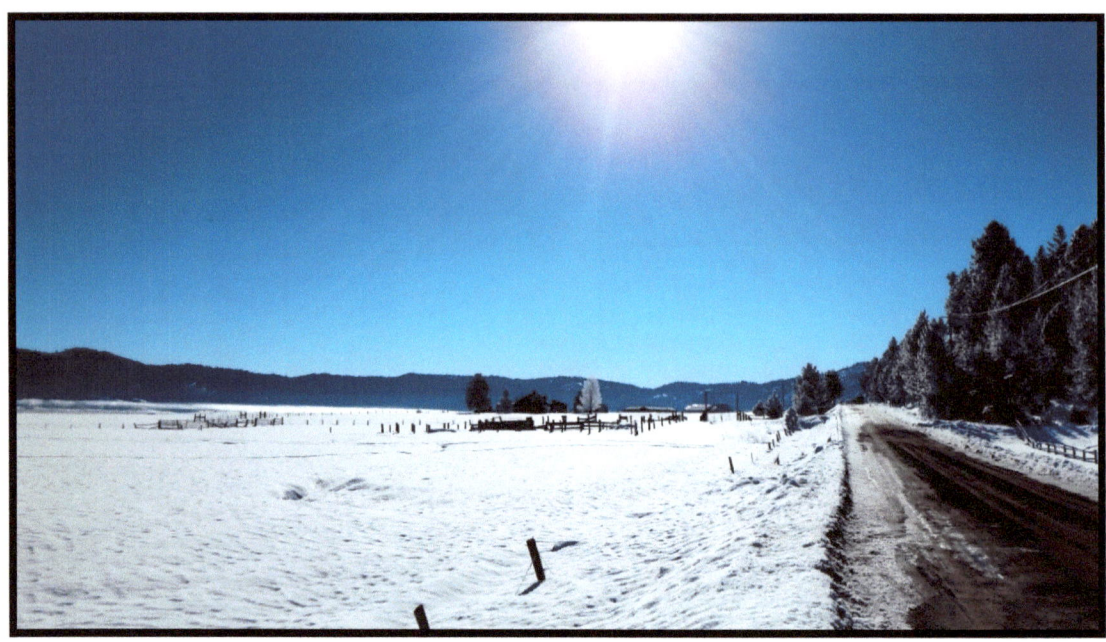

The Sun lights up the Land near the Boise National forest.

As the Valley wakes up early morning to hear,
the Deer rustle in the Forest
while they are looking for wild Berries to eat.

Mountains and the Flatlands

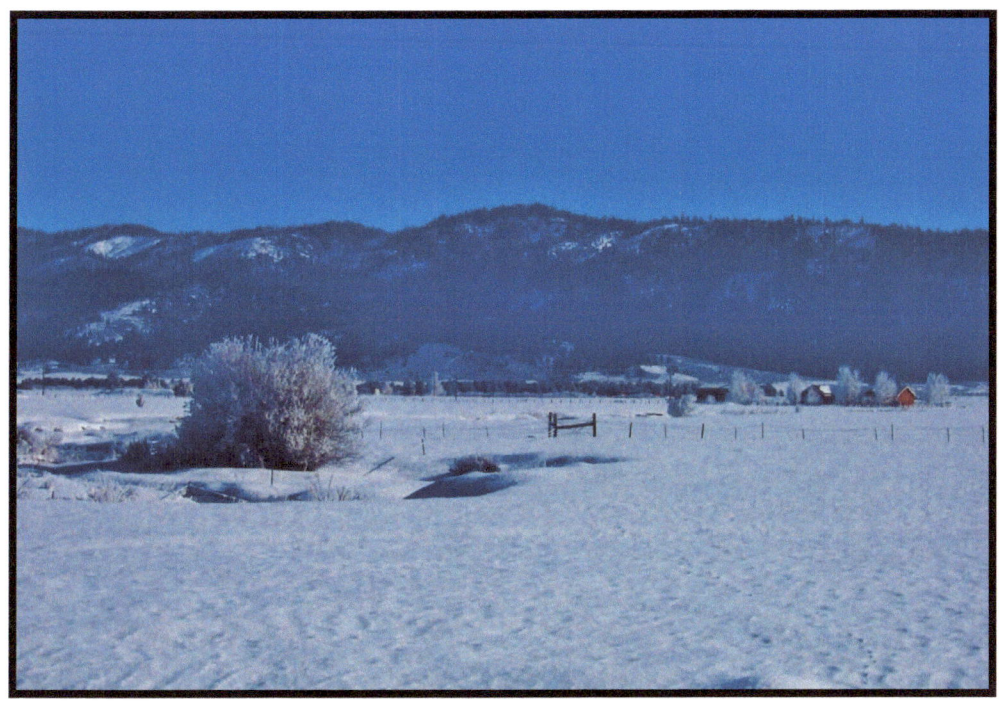

Oh' she cried out with a voice.

How great is our Creator of the Universe

to give us such Divine beauty in Idaho?

Great and Majestic is our God!

Ranches and Snow

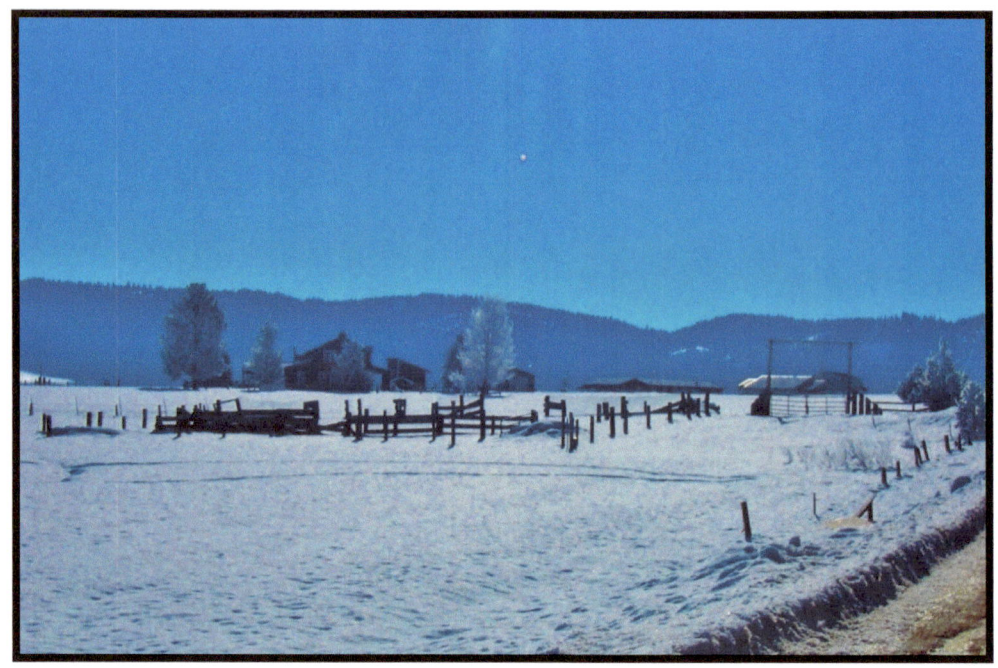

The Moon tells her Story of the Beauty

in a far away land.

As the Trees, give Ear to hear her Voice

in the Stillness of the day.

As the Settlers are in their Houses asleep she

continues up the Road looking at the snow.

Shadows of the Forest

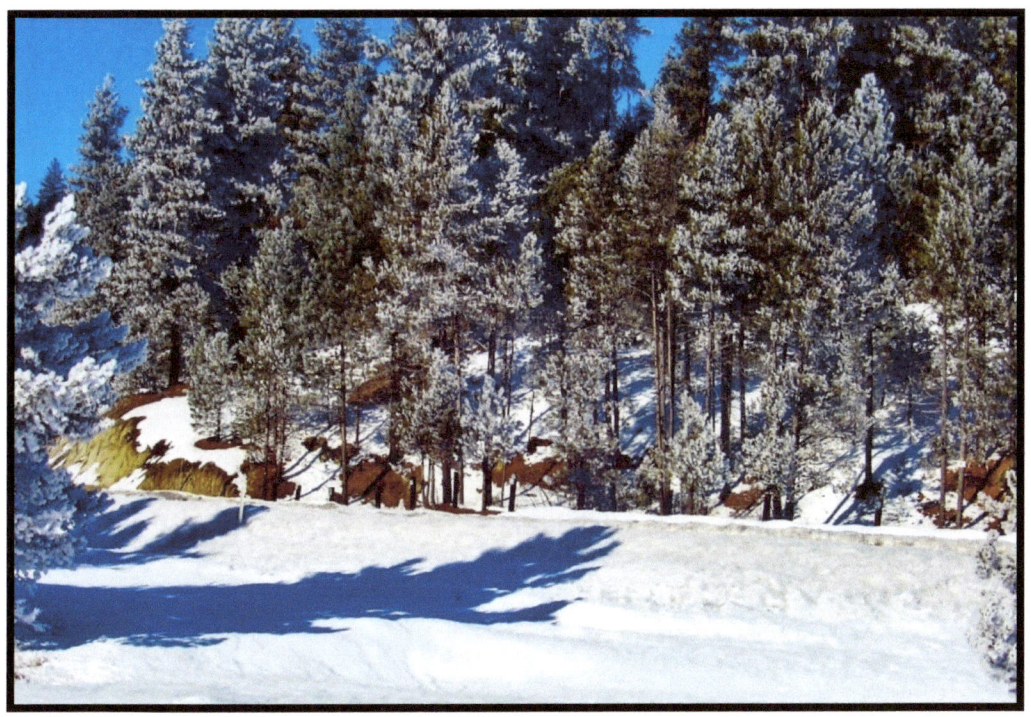

Red Rock in formation along the path of a

Highway leading into the Boise National forest of pristine beauty

One enjoyed on a Warm and Sunny day.

Beauty in Winter

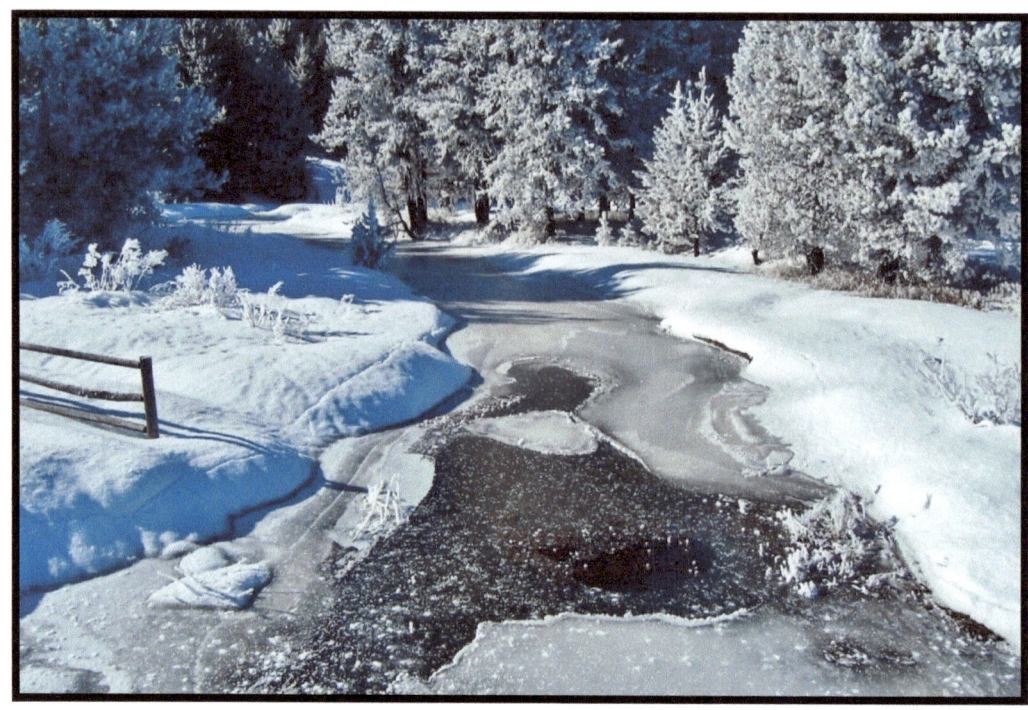

River of Beauty

Magical Snow covered the Pine Trees

Wooden Fence

Valley of pureness

Untouched

Snow and Frozen River

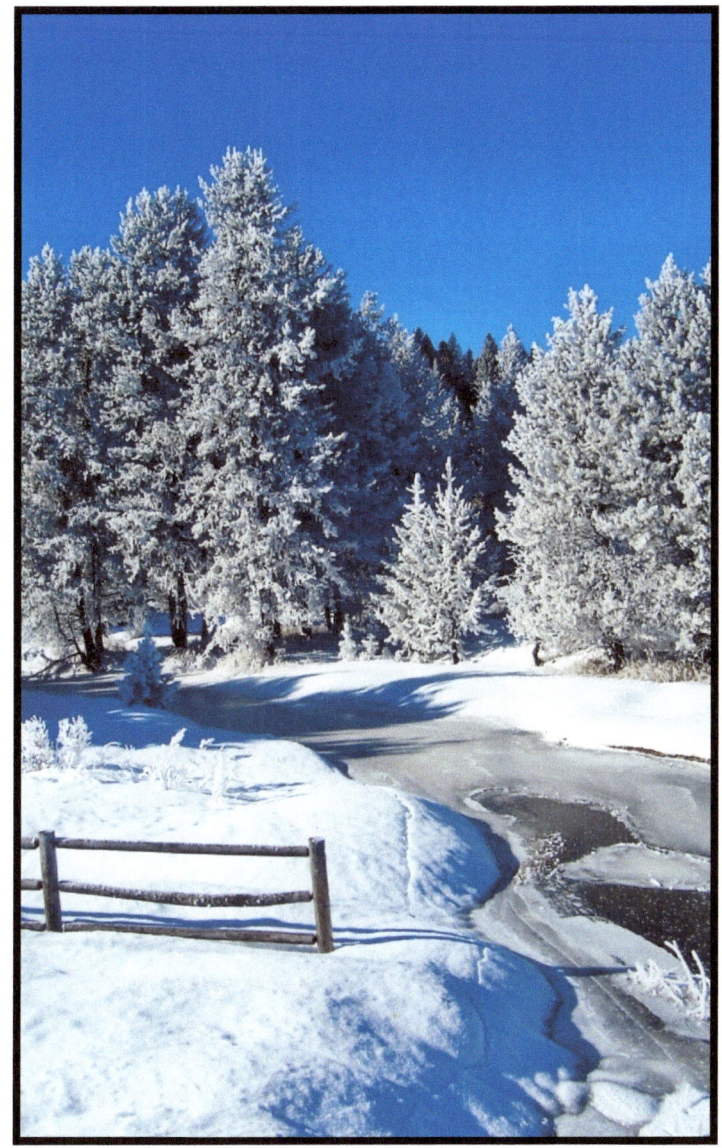

Creamy and Smooth Snow on the land

Frozen River in Winter Season

Cascades and Settlers Cabin

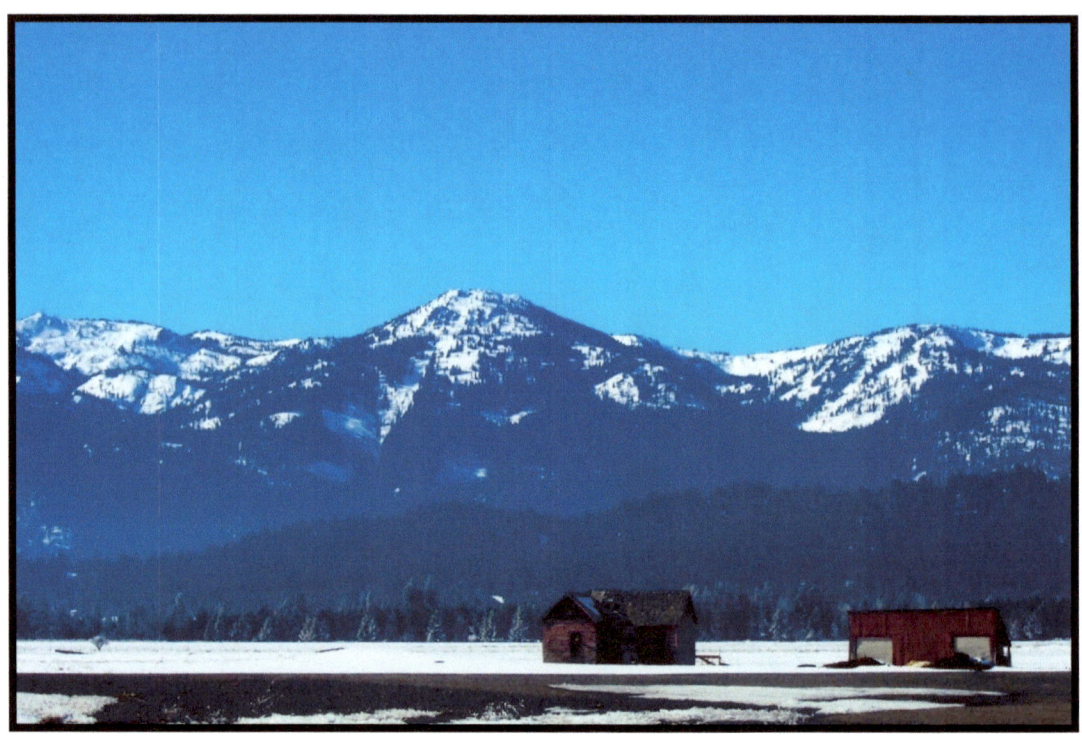

Majestic Beauty

Secrets of the Mountains

Valley of Forest Trees

Settlers Cabin

Tool Shed

Forest Trees and Snow on Land

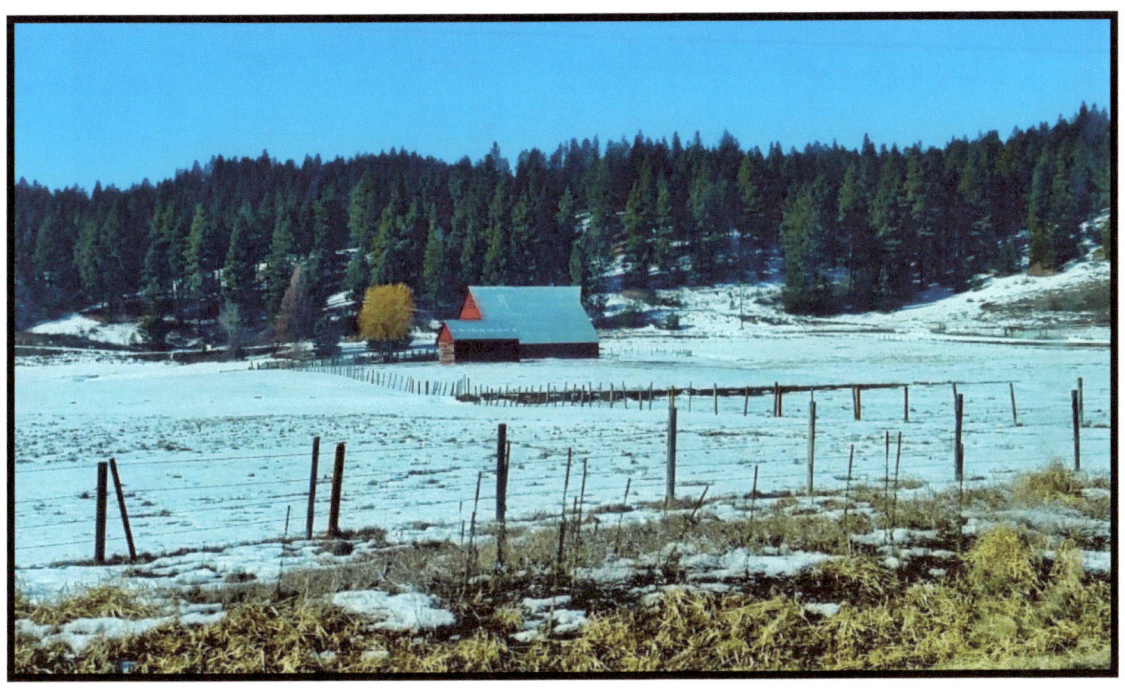

Red Barn and Tool Crib

Fences outstretched

A Valley of Forest Trees among a golden tree

Open Range

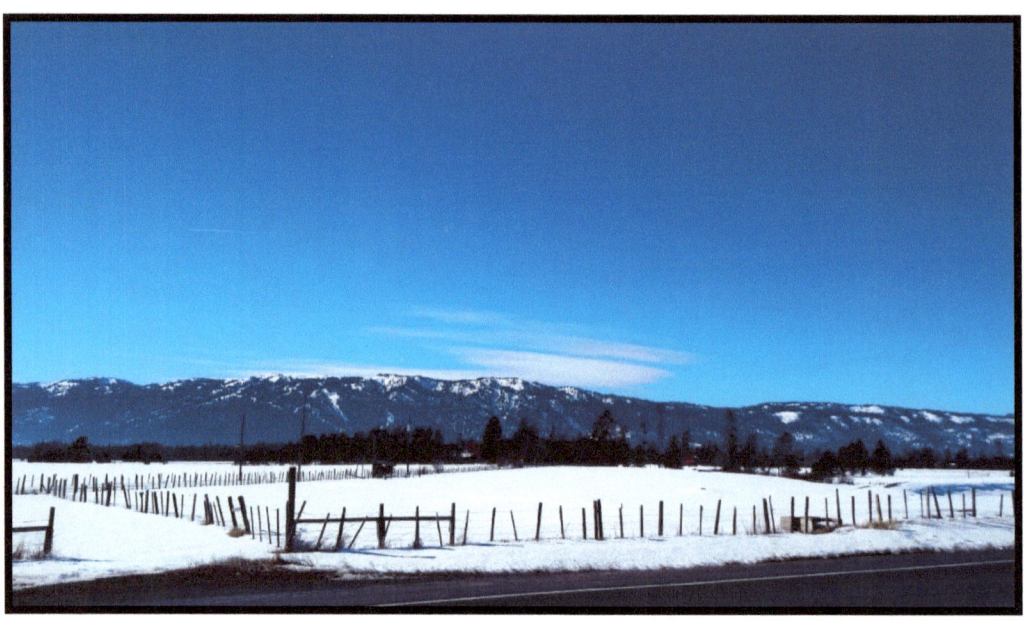

Cascade Range

Wooden Fences

Pine Trees

Valley of Stillness

Tree Shadows among the Barns

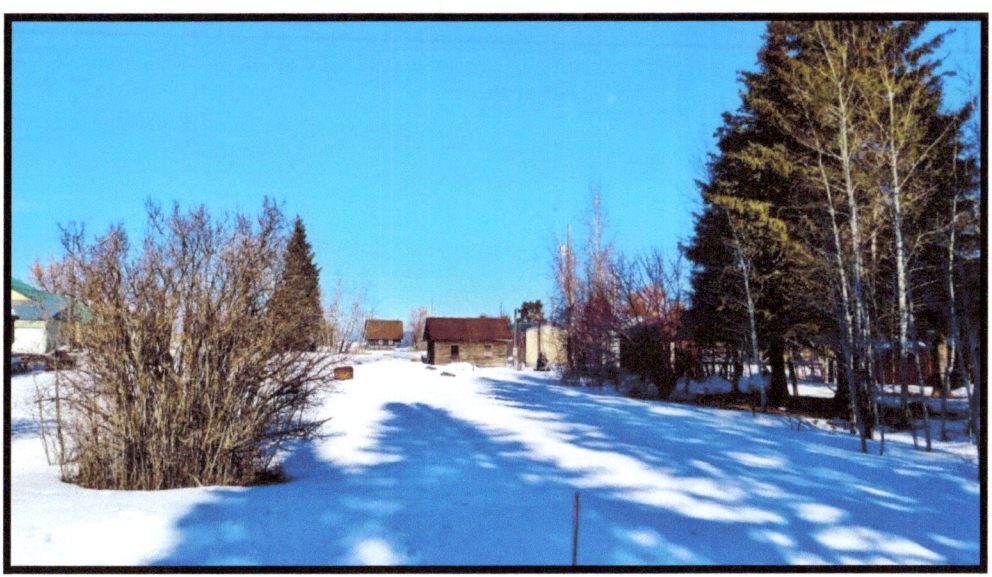

Shadows on the Trees

Sunlight Reflections

Abandoned Cabin and Sheds

Stillness

Pine Trees

Wooden Fence and Houses

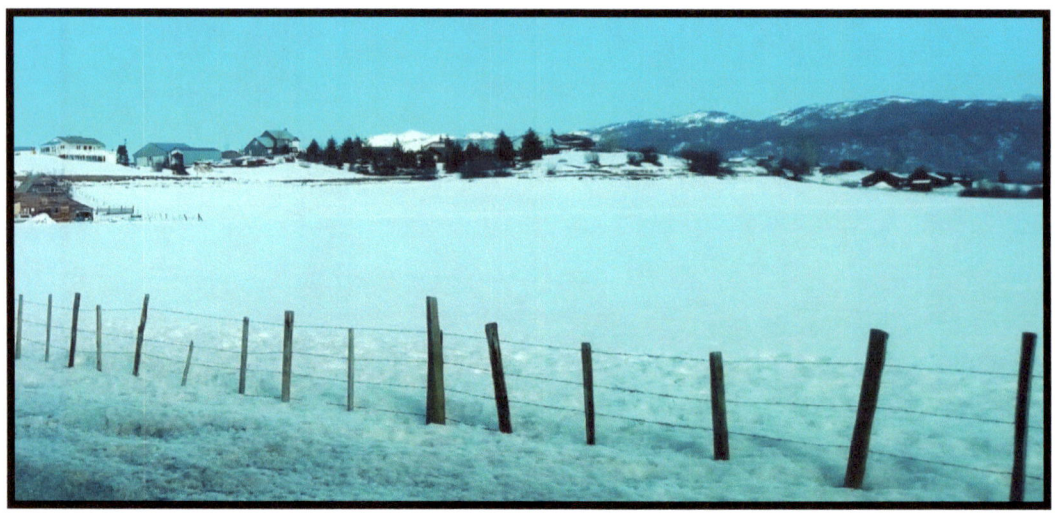

In the distance, one could see Snow on the Mountains.

There are Blue and Gray colored painted houses within view.

A Vintage Truck and Farming Equipment off to the left side

are on the land.

Stillness in Pure Beauty is divine.

Just Around the Bend

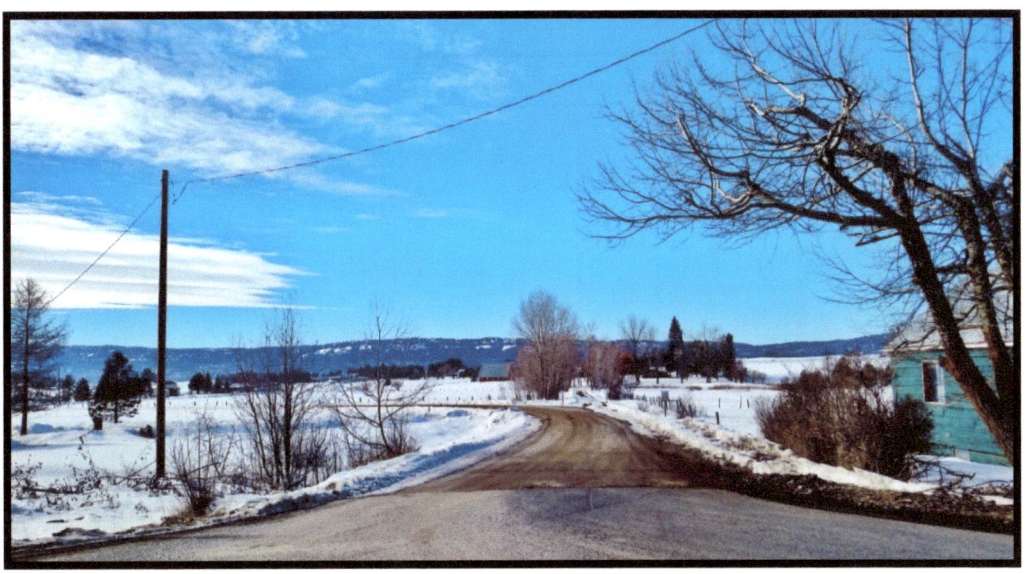

Aqua painted colored wooden House

Oak and Pine Trees

Telephone Poles

Rustic Barns in the distance

Beauty

Pioneer Log Cabin

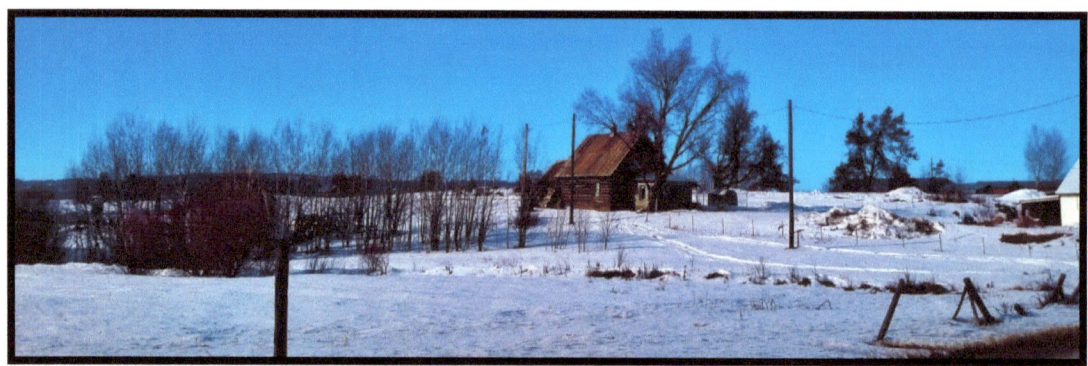

Cabin

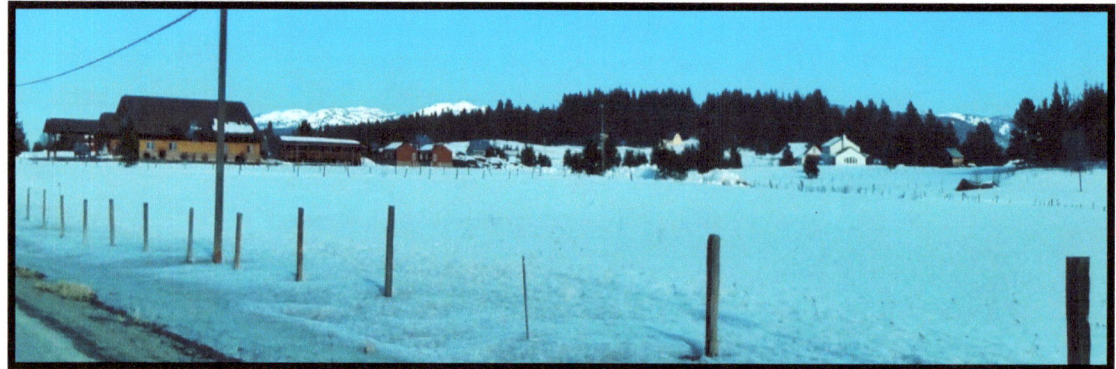

School House and Country Houses

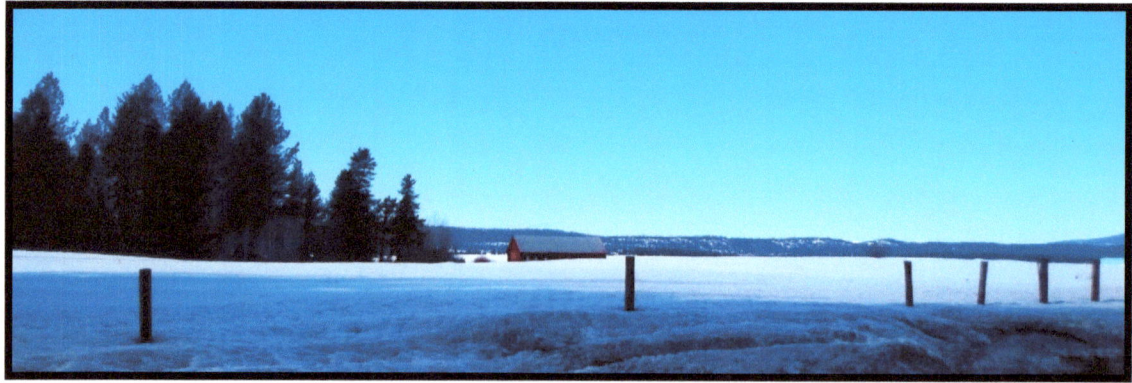

Red Barn

The Valley

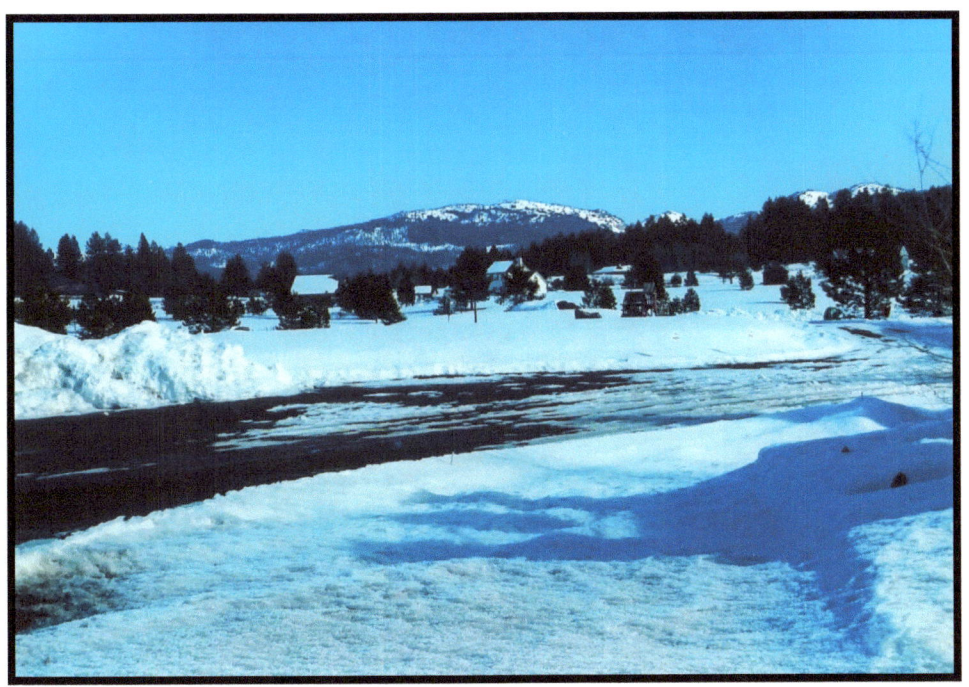

Village of Houses

People nesting

during Winter Season

The Valley is filled with ice on the roads,

and in the distance you can hear

the Snowplows trying to make their way to clear the roads.

Red Barn in McCall

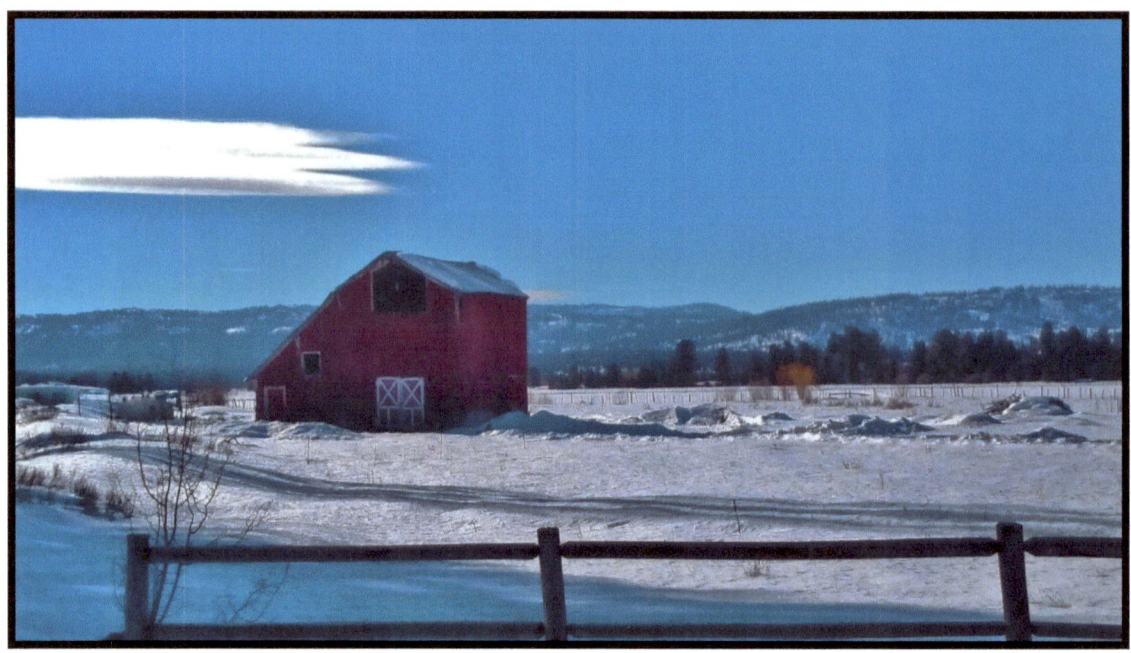

Throughout the McCall, area is numerous Rustic Barns on farms.

The view of the Cascades and Mountains are breathtaking to witness.

There are Wooden fences along many paths leading to private

Properties and vast land of many Pine trees.

Ice-Skaters

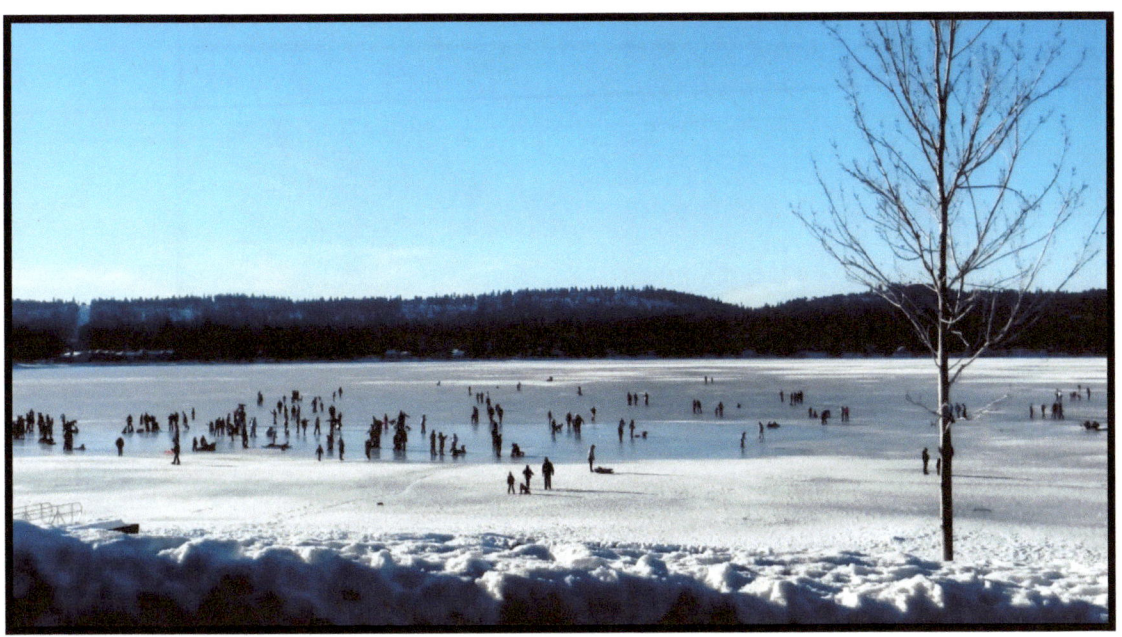

The Ice-Skaters are out with their family and friends

on a brisk early morning in McCall, Idaho.

The area is considered a wonderful place for travelers and vacationers

for its natural beauty.

The community holds annual events throughout the year.

There are Cabins in the area and places to Fish,

in addition, a nearby Ski Resort in the mountains.

Some people stay on their Houseboats to reside and enjoy

the tranquil way of life.

Beauty of Landscapes

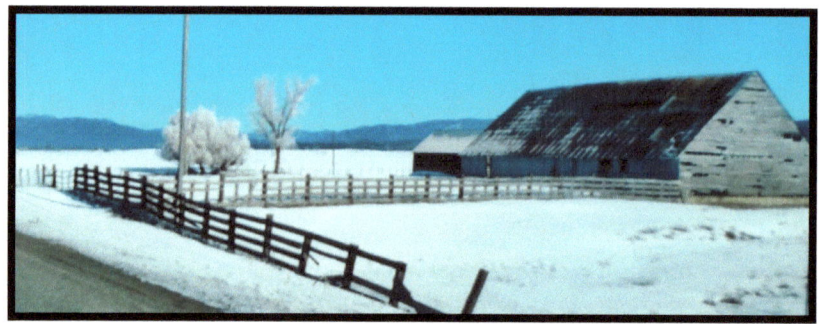

Barns and Farms

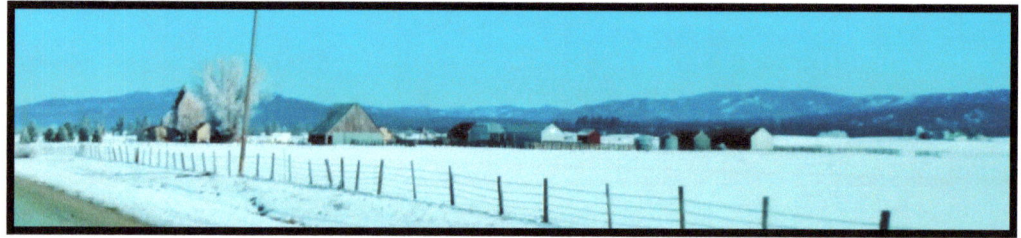

Wooden Fences

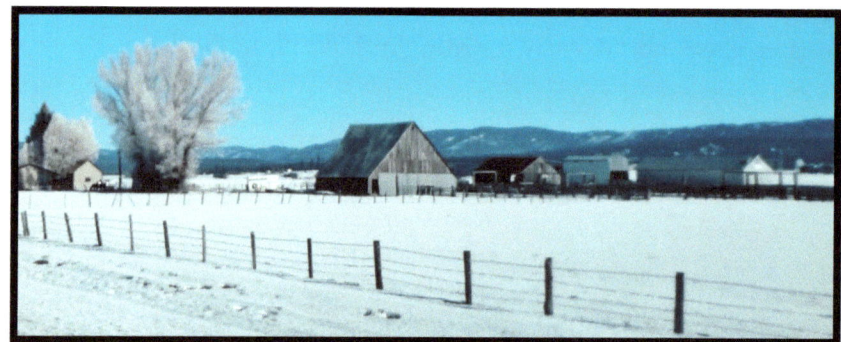

Oak Tree with Frost

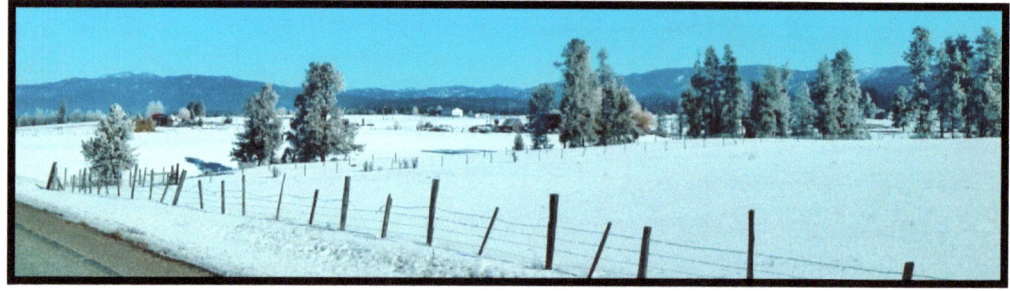

Corral and Snow-Capped Mountains

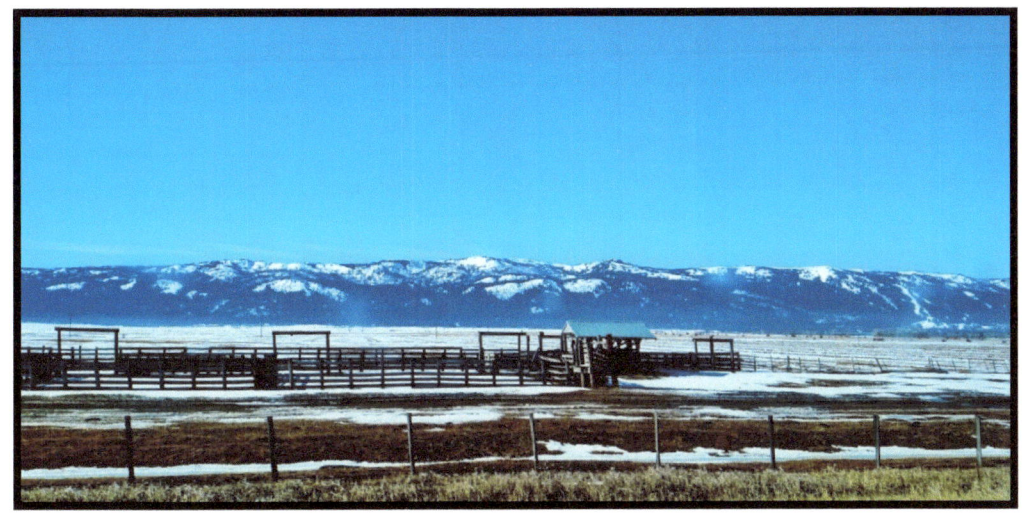

The Corral

a place the Cowboys

Ride their American Quarter Horses

to brand the Cattle with a mark

of ownership and have a Thermos filled with

Hot Coffee, and perhaps a Teaspoon of Whiskey to keep

from the winters, chill.

Tranquil Beauty

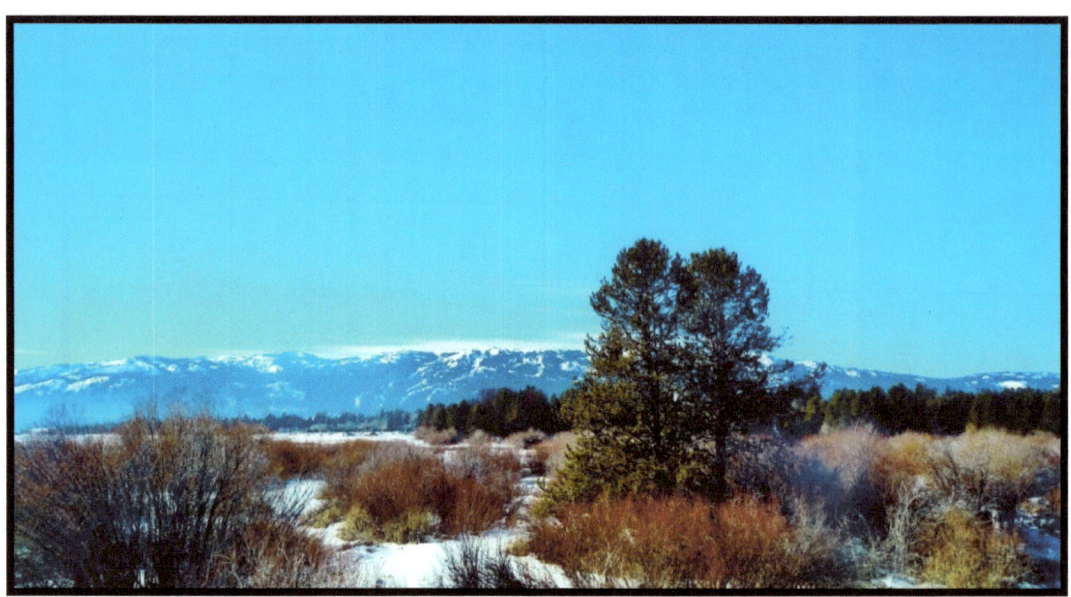

Blue Sky

Green and tall Pine Trees along

Wild brush in Burnt Umber, and gold.

Squirrels and a Red Fox are seen

Running from hiding while weaving

in, and out of its open paths.

They both then stop to Feast upon the land.

Tree Branches and Blue Sky

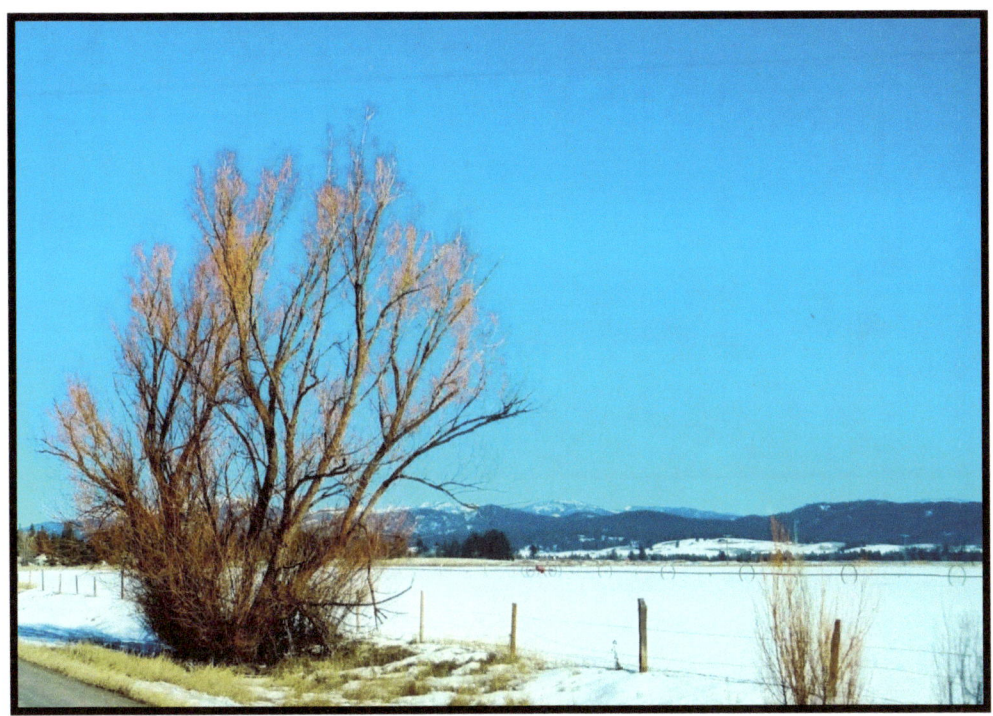

Outstretched Tree Branches

Yielding to the Beauty of the

Land and the Hillsides on a clear day.

Heading Out on the Open Road

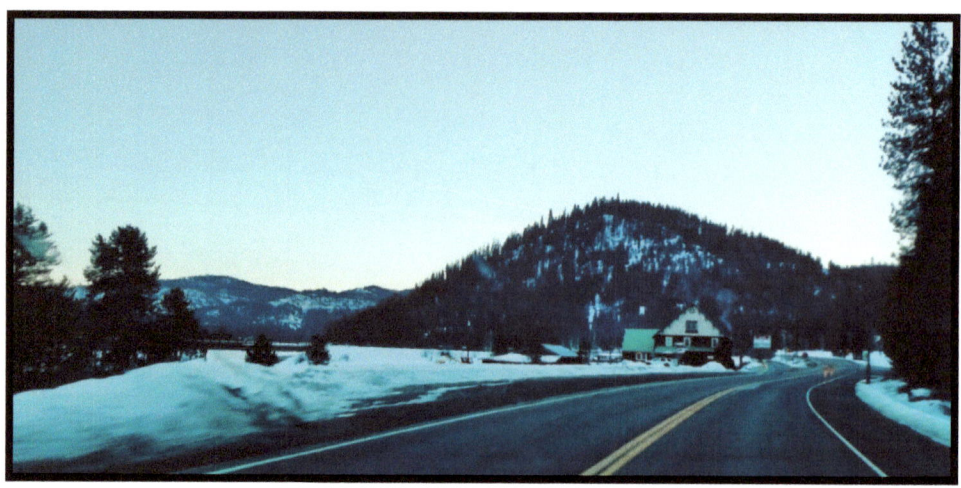

Heading back from McCall, Idaho into

the Boise National Forest is a sight to see.

While remembering the Snow-Capped Mountains and Hillsides

with natural Beauty, and the Cascades.

The open Plains filled with Rustic Barns and Wooden Fences

from Settlers who built them, and Homesteaded in the vast area

was amazing to experience.

Including, all the Urban City and Country Folks who

Seek to have a glimpse of what it is like to take in the beauty of Idaho.

Many people come just for the enjoyment of the Mountains, Fishing, Kayaking, Hiking,

Boating, River rafting, and Motocross riding in the Hills or Snow-Skiing at the resorts.

In addition, many Artists come to Plein Air Paint outdoors

and Writers who come to stay in Cabin retreats.

The great State of Idaho is a well-kept secret and as word, spreads among people more individuals are coming to the area for retirement, and others make it a place for future travels here within the United States of America.

Literary Published Works
Peggy Leyva Conley

Books

The Grandeur Beauty of Idaho
Photography – Poetry – Published 2017

The Essence of Expression
Poetry and Quotes - Published 2017

Life Philosophy through Nature
Poetry - Spirituality – Photography – Published 2017

Southern Roots Cookbook
Clark-Manning Families
Appalachian Mountains of Eastern Tennessee
Recipes-Genealogy-History-Photography – Published 2016

Petarchian Sonnets-Italian
Poetry – Drawings and Photography
Published 2016

American Sonnets
Poetry-Photography – Published 2016

Poetic Visions and Paintings
Art-Poetry-Quotes -Published 2016

The Potter and Sculptress
Clay/Ceramic Wheel Throwing/Hand Designs – Published 2016

Landscape Paintings and Haiku Poetry
Coastlines-Mountains-Terrain – Published 2016

Vibrant Flowers and Garden
Painting-Drawings – Published 2016

Drawing and Paintings
Poetry – Published 2016

Nature Calling
Photography-Poetry – Published 2016

Winter Season with Nature – Landscape Scenes
Poetry and Photography - Published 2016

Life in the Country – White Cotton Sheets
Poetry and Photography – Published 2016

At the Heart of Aromatherapy – Nature Botanicals
Herbs – Soaps – Oils – Fragrance – Published 2016

The Transcendental Zen Garden
Poetry and Photography – Published 2016

Poetic Inspirations
Poetry and Photography – Published 2016

Discography - Music

Passages of Time

(Classical: Film Music) - Released 2010

Canterbury Manor
(Classical: Chamber Music) – Released 2013

Ancient Garden of Knowledge
(Classical: Orchestral) – Released 2013

Midnight Telephone Blues
(Blues: Delta Style) - Released 2013

In the Face of Blues
(Acoustic Blues) – Released 2013

Mountain Blues
(Acoustic Blues) – Released 2013

Available on International Distribution